~~never again!~~

A PERSONAL STRUGGLE WITH THE HOLOCAUST AND GENOCIDE

yet again!

~~never again!~~

A PERSONAL STRUGGLE WITH THE HOLOCAUST AND GENOCIDE

yet again!

Stephen D. Smith

~~never again!~~ yet again!
A PERSONAL STRUGGLE WITH THE HOLOCAUST AND GENOCIDE

by Stephen D. Smith

Published in Israel by
Gefen Publishing House Ltd.
6 Hatzvi St, Jerusalem, 94386, Israel

© 2009 Stephen D. Smith
First published in Israel, 2009

British Library Catalogue in Publication Data
A catalogue record for this book is available from the British Library.

ISBN 978-965-229-491-3

All rights reserved. No part of this publication may be reproduced in any form or by any means, electronic, mechanical, photocopying, recording or otherwise, without the prior permission of the author.

Cover Photograph: Stephen and James Smith by Nathanael Boarer
Design and artwork by Glen Powell, The Holocaust Centre

To Jackie
Who had no idea just how much she would change my life.
"What shall I do now?"

TABLE OF CONTENTS

Acknowledgments *ix*

Introduction *xi*

PART I – DISCOVERIES

Chapter One: The Trip to Jerusalem *1*

Chapter Two: (My) Trip to Jerusalem *5*

Chapter Three: House of Peace *11*

Chapter Four: Discovering the Jewish Tradition *15*

Chapter Five: Jim and I *21*

Chapter Six: Confronting the Holocaust *25*

Chapter Seven: Where Memories Meet *41*

PART II – DECISIONS

Chapter Eight: Making Memory	*61*
Chapter Nine: Vision to Reality	*75*
Chapter Ten: In the Public Eye	*85*
Chapter Eleven: From Past to Future	*89*

PART III – REFLECTIONS

Chapter Twelve: Legacies	*105*
Chapter Thirteen: Landscapes of Memory	*111*
Chapter Fourteen: The Jewish-Christian Relationship	*123*
Chapter Fifteen: The Holocaust and the Future of Western Civilization	*129*
Chapter Sixteen: What Next?	*145*
Chapter Seventeen: The Journey	*153*
Chapter Eighteen: A Girl Called Irene	*159*
Chapter Nineteen: ~~Never Again!~~ Yet Again!	*185*
Chapter Twenty: The Future of Memory	*195*
Chapter Twenty-One: Inconclusive	*201*

Acknowledgments

To all those people who have enriched me, guided me, listened to me, criticized me, and made me stronger, more determined than ever.

There are too many to mention. But I cannot let the moment pass without saying a huge thank-you to my brother, James, who has been my collaborator since we were children – and always will be. To my parents, Marina and Eddie, who have supported our efforts without complaint. To my children, Natalia, Stephanie, and Aaron, who never stop reminding me what a great gift life really is! To Heather, who has inspired me all over again. To the amazing staff of the Holocaust Centre in England and Aegis Trust around the world, without whom this would not have been possible. To friends who have encouraged me, pushed me back, made me think, and re-think. Above all, I want to pay tribute to the team of Holocaust survivors in the United Kingdom, who have been there for me, working tirelessly, on behalf of all of us. To all of you who have encouraged me and let me share in your life, thank you. And to all those who have put up with my energy and seen each deadline as a useful challenge, thank you.

Introduction

Every day – yes, that's every day – someone somewhere asks me to explain how a family with no connection to the Holocaust came to start Britain's first dedicated Holocaust memorial and education center. Now I get asked how an Englishman who is not Jewish has ended up running the Shoah Foundation Institute in Los Angeles, the most significant visual history archive of Holocaust survivor testimony. Good questions that demand thorough answers.

    I hope this book will go some way to answering those questions. It will hopefully explain the journey I have taken into dark memory to try to create a way to express ourselves in the shadow of such a demanding history. I have tried to keep my comments and insights as brief as possible. It is autobiographical in style as it is the only way to tell this story. I hope I have not been too personal in the process, but it was a personal journey so that is how I have told it. Because of its content, this book is not just for reading, but also for sharing. I hope it will inspire us all to continue our efforts to commemorate the victims of the Holocaust, and to create a world in which the potential for repetition of such inhumanity is greatly reduced.

Stephen D. Smith
September 2009

PART ONE
DISCOVERIES

PART ONE – DISCOVERIES

CHAPTER ONE
THE TRIP TO JERUSALEM

There is a tiny public house in Nottingham that claims to be Britain's smallest tavern. Its beer tastes much the same as everywhere else in the world; its wine cellar is too small to be a connoisseur's paradise, but it is not a place for the connoisseur, but rather the tourist. It has the rather quaint name "The Trip to Jerusalem." Its twisted oak beams and tiny bar are cut into the rock directly under the imposing walls of Nottingham Castle. It is quaint and ominous. Such cute antiquity casts a long, dark shadow across Europe's history. "The Trip to Jerusalem" it describes was no vacation, but of course the bloody visit of the Crusades to the Holy Land. Nottingham Castle perches high on a sandstone outcrop right in the center of the city. It has been there since the mythical stories of local hero Robin Hood were first whispered among the peasants of the time.

Some of my first memories are of Sherwood Forest and the tree said to have been inhabited by Robin Hood and his merry men – like the day we went on a woodland walk in the forest when I was in first grade. We managed to get the whole class of twenty-five children inside the hollow trunk of the great Sherwood Oak. Even as a six-year-old, it did cross my mind that it would have been a much smaller tree 850 years earlier, and may not have been big enough for all the merry men. But the teachers

~~Never Again!~~ Yet Again!

seemed convinced that the whole band of outlaws had crammed onto its then sapling branches. Who was I to argue?

It all sounds idyllic – castles, taverns, oak forests. But don't be misled. Just as "Bethlehem" might remind you of mangers, shepherds, lowing cattle, and angels – until you say "Bethlehem, Pennsylvania" – so, too, Sherwood Forest may conjure up images of leafy forest, with sunlight dropping golden through bright green foliage, and outlaws shuffling through the undergrowth, the king's stag slung between their shoulders. That is, until you say, Thoresby coal mine, Ollerton coal mine, Rufford coal mine, Bilsthorpe, Blidworth, Rainworth, Mansfield, Ashfield, and Bevercotes too! Somehow there is coal right underneath Sherwood Forest and every village had a soot-black pit and ugly, grey winding gear. Small rural villages had been replaced with larger industrial villages.

I peered through the coal dust coating my bedroom window to the slag heap behind the house. The wheels of the winding gear were doing their usual high-speed spin, bringing up the next load of weary miners. I wondered which of my friends' dads were coming up or going down. There was a bit of a commotion in the garden; some kids in my mother's youth group were arguing about something rather loudly. Cigarettes? Pulling up the vegetables again? Fighting? Drugs? It would definitely be one of them. I squinted to see who was in trouble this time. I so wanted to go down and join the big kids. But I was only seven years old and had been sent to bed early. They were sixteen-year-olds, many with criminal records. My brother James and I were always banished to our bedrooms on youth group night, with pouting faces pushed against the dusty glass.

My dad was unusual among the other dads in my class. He did go down the pit – but just once, to visit! Everyone else's dad went down pretty much every day. Men went to work down the pit. Women in the hosiery mills. That was how it worked. My best friend Paddle had a dad who was a pit manager. He took my dad on a visit. Unlike most of the people in the village, we were not living there because of coal. We were there because of religion – Methodist Christianity to be more precise.

The Trip to Jerusalem

I sometimes trudged and sometimes skipped happily along Forest Road to the Methodist church. I knew the five-minute route well. At the time, it did not occur to me that there was no forest at either end of Forest Road. The routine was pretty straightforward – church, school, bible study, more school, junior youth group, yet more school, and even more church. The cycle was pretty well set so that nothing would change.

Chapter Two
(My) Trip to Jerusalem

Evening sunlight still heats cold stone in Jerusalem. It absorbs orange light, dragging it into itself, warming cool buff to gold. The soft shuffle of feet and the quiet echo of distant prayer, muffled by silence and the beat of pigeons' wings, were eerily unique, but enticing nevertheless. There were no walls, no roof, no altar, yet clearly it was a sacred place. Just an empty space, open to the skies and an old wall of huge stones. Yet there was a strange sense of the divine. I listened to the tip-tap of shoes close by, making their way towards the ancient stones. They clipped along, quieter and quieter, till they were drowned out by the tin yell of *Allahu Akbar* bouncing off the same stone, loud, penetrating. I wanted to touch those huge stones. I felt the urge to touch history, to mingle among the sounds of prayer lost in the flap of pigeon wings and the shuffle of feet on their way to and from meeting their God. It was the first time I had encountered history and tradition bound together like that, other than on infrequent visits to echoing, cold cathedrals back in England. As I stood there, huge blocks towered above me. How did I know that they were sacred? Maybe it was the setting, maybe the people milling around, maybe the Hasidim bobbing up and down, *peyes* swinging in rhythm to their prayers. Maybe it was the silence, the prayers, and the scale of those huge blocks put together.

~~Never Again!~~ Yet Again!

Whatever its origin, I could feel their challenge, their sanctity, and their power. It was possibly the most important day of my life – I just did not know it then.

I was just thirteen years old at the time. It was 1981. I had been brought up in a home where Christianity played a central, if not the only, role. My parents, Eddie and Marina, and my younger brother James and I were standing at the back of the plaza in Jerusalem where the Western Wall, the *Kotel*, is situated. We were very excited, if a little overawed, at being there. Yet we did not really know quite what we were looking at, or why it seemed so impressive. Nor did we know what to do once we got there. We ventured forward from the back of the plaza and approached the wall. Mother went right to go to the ladies' section. We three "men" stood looking over the fence for some time at the comings and goings of Jewish men praying at the wall. It was Friday afternoon – *Erev Shabbat*. We had no idea what was going on. We knew that Saturday was the Sabbath. We had also been warned that Jewish festivals begin the evening before. But we did not realize that there was a long build-up to Friday night, and that the mass of activity down at the wall was largely related to this.

The three of us obediently put on those paper *yarmulkes* that the man at the gate hands out if you try to enter without a head covering. Father, James and I walked up and stood by the wall, peering across to see if we could see Mother over the *mehitza* dividing the men from the women. I remember looking at the deeply riven surface of the stones, examining their texture, wondering if it had always been like that, or whether it had weathered over time. Close up, it no longer seemed like an oversized garden wall with little ant-like people milling around its base. It was imposing, eternal and immovable. As I stood there, I tried to pray something, but did not quite know what to pray. I was intrigued by the bits of paper with prayers written on them – *kvitlach* – which were stuffed into the joints of the blocks. I was momentarily tempted to take one out to see what was written on it. Instead, I found myself staring at the gnarled stone a few inches away from my nose, with a question floating around my head. "How is it that we come to this beautiful old city to learn something about the origins of our Christianity and yet, when we see a part of that, as Judaism is being practiced here today, we don't know what is happening?" I queried further, "Why not? Aren't these Jewish people praying at the site of the Temple where Jesus of Nazareth came to pray as a Jew? Aren't they saying the same prayers? If I consider myself a follower of that same Jesus, shouldn't I understand something of what is happening here?"

Of course, I was too young to formulate those particular questions in that particular way, but they indicate the essence of what I was thinking. As I look back and try to remember the sensation of standing there, can I say for certain that those would have been the questions to emerge from the confusing buzz in my head if I had known how to ask them? I knew that I wanted to understand the connection between Judaism and Christianity, between them and me, between past and present. I did know that there was something missing in my knowledge. I knew that I had lots of questions and wanted to know the answers. What I do remember is this: I was so absorbed in what was happening that I didn't want to leave. I felt that hidden there, somewhere in that stone wall, was a dimension of my life that I had yet to explore. And I wanted to know more.

That was in March 1981. I was going to turn fourteen in April. James, my brother, was nearly twelve years old. The family holiday to Israel was more of an adventure for us than anything else. It was a chance to explore the world in a new way, to discover new people and places. Unlike a lot of children these days who take flying for granted, this was the first time we had been on an airplane. Our previous forays abroad as a family had always been by car to the European continent. This alone made the journey more memorable. Friends of my mother and father had parents living in the Jerusalem neighborhood of Ramat Eshkol, and so we arrived and spent the week with the Backhouse family. Through their hospitality, operating out of their apartment, we went out each day to explore the city.

~~Never Again!~~ Yet Again!

My parents had made a wise decision not to go on an organized Holy Land Tour, bumping around the countryside in a sweaty bus with nattering evangelical Christians. Instead, they chose to explore the sights and sounds of Israel on our own do-it-yourself tour. We were there as a Christian family learning about the Holy Land and the meaning of its history and culture for us. Like many of the hundreds of thousands of people who have clambered onto chartered flights at Gatwick Airport, we expected to go there and return enriched, having discovered more about the origins of our religious tradition. We expected to have things confirmed, underscored, explained, and clarified. Much of what we experienced was confirming. Having just finished the interminable round of Sunday-school stories from the New Testament, I felt there was something captivating about standing on the site where the Feeding of the Five Thousand was said to have happened, or where John the Baptist is said to have baptized Jesus. However, very quickly we discovered a complex, diverse, and challenging Israel, which we had not bargained for. I don't think we made much sense of that complexity there and then. But I do distinctly remember feeling more and more inquisitive about the ancient history of Jerusalem and its meaning for the Jewish people.

We hired a caravan on the shores of Lake Kinneret and explored the region around the lake, going into the Golan during our second week. Much of our time was spent quietly by the lakeside. It was March and the tourist season was yet to get underway, and so we almost had the whole place to ourselves. From time to time, Mother sat by the beach and talked to us as we threw stones into the lake or idly tried to catch the small fish darting around the rocks. She told me that all over Israel, Jewish boys of my age had just completed their bar mitzvah and were now considered men in their communities. I guess I was a little envious that they had the opportunity to become recognized as being grown up so young. As we continued to plop stones into the water, we talked about the importance of making the right personal choices as adults, of taking responsibility for our own actions, and being independent in our social, moral, religious and spiritual convictions. She talked about the need to know who you are, what you are doing, and the importance of following your own convictions. A teenage lecture. On reflection, those moments of discussion helped shape and guide the way choices were made thereafter, when I made some of the more challenging decisions later in my life.

As James and I focused on catching the fish zipping between our legs, we had just started on a long and exciting journey of discovery, although of course we still did not know that then.

CHAPTER THREE
HOUSE OF PEACE

Some days are more significant than others. March 4, 1978, turned out to be a big day in our lives. I was eleven years old when my parents decided to make a courageous career change. Until then, my father had been a minister in the Methodist Church and my mother was a secondary-school teacher, teaching religious education. I remember quite distinctly the day that things changed. I had been up early that morning to go on a school trip to Wembley soccer stadium to see England's schoolboys play the schoolboys of France. Growing up in the North Nottinghamshire coal-mining village of Ollerton, this was a big day in my life. The fact that England lost to the French did not seem to spoil the excitement of traveling to London, and all the fun that went with it. By the time I came home, I had acquired an England hat and scarf and a France rosette with *Le Coq Sportif* printed in the middle of it. My friend Adrian Singleton's father came with us. He teased us all by supporting France throughout, which made us all both hopping mad and hilariously happy. Naturally, I returned home early that evening bursting to tell my parents about my great adventure. I started telling them about the huge stadium and about Adrian's father buying a France rosette to goad us with and, of course, showing off my England scarf. However, I had hardly started when my parents said they had something very important to discuss with me.

We sat down on those rather rough, hard settees in the lounge, the ones with the prickly fabric, and Mother carefully explained

~~Never Again!~~ Yet Again!

that she and my father had decided they wanted to start a charitable trust and buy a house where they could make their work in the Christian Church more meaningful. They planned to create a house, like a small conference center or place of retreat, where people could come to study, to learn, or to be quiet and reflect. They explained that they felt it was one thing working in the Christian Church, but it was another living a Christian life, and they felt they could best fulfill this by serving society in a broader way.

Apparently, they wanted to find a more meaningful way of making the Christian message work in everyday life. They went on to explain that they had very little money to achieve this goal and so it might not happen, but that they were going to hand in their resignations at their respective places of work. They wanted my brother and me to make the decision with them as it would inevitably have a radical impact on our lives, and we should choose to do it together as a family, or not at all.

It is strange, but both James and I readily agreed to this plan, even though it seemed to entail the possibility of a move away from friends, school, and all the things that give you security as young children. I remember being impressed with their bravery and being involved in the conversation, as this was clearly a risky thing to do. I don't remember too much about the following six months, except that my parents were searching for properties, looking worried from time to time and praying like crazy for funding for the project. There were several false dawns and, as the year wore on, the chances of finding a place were getting slimmer. The clock was running down, too, because the house we were living in was owned by their now previous employer, who had another minister of religion arriving on September 1st. There was talk of living on the streets – or worse, with Grandma! Notwithstanding the humor, they were running a risk, but it was one they felt they had to take. Indeed, it was a chance they were convinced they should take. You learn a lot from that as an eleven-year-old boy, perched on the edge of your seat, pretending not to understand what is happening around you.

House of Peace

Just in time in August, they purchased a very old-looking, run-down farmhouse in the middle of the countryside, about a mile from the village of Laxton. It fitted their meager budget of £25,000, but really the place was in need of a lot of attention by that time. It had started life as a late-Victorian farmhouse on Thoresby Estate, built for the then Lady Manvers. It had been occupied by the tenant farmer and workers until the developing age of mechanization had made its use redundant. And so, over a number of years, it had fallen into disrepair. My parents' friends shook their heads in dismay as they heard that Mother and Father were moving into such a place with two young children. The roof had huge holes in it, water was running down the inside walls and the place had to be entirely rewired, plumbed, and virtually re-roofed before the winter set in.

I remember clearly the discussion that revolved around the naming of this new place. Various ideas were discussed that would appeal to what would be a largely Christian clientele. I remember that most, if not all, of the alternatives were Greek in derivation, chosen for their New Testament links. But one option developed which was Hebrew in origin: "*Shalom*... peace, or... why not house of peace?" went the conversation. Although both of my parents had studied theology at college, neither had learned Hebrew formally, but they knew enough to know that *Beth El* was "House of God," so by deduction, *Beth Shalom* would probably mean "House of Peace." "*Beth Shalom*, yes, *Beth Shalom* seems good." And so, even though the vast majority of Christians coming to the place would not recognize what it meant, and with absolutely no other Hebrew in our lives, we moved into our *Beth Shalom*.

It was a strange existence really. Exciting, too. There was constant banging, hammering, and the grinding of brick dust. Winter came, and predictably the house still had no central heating. I suppose as youngsters we saw it as a great adventure, but it really was quite cold. It happened to be the winter in which snowdrifts piled up high, and temperatures of -12 degrees centigrade (10 Fahrenheit) were a common feature. Another family

~~Never Again!~~ Yet Again!

had moved into the house too, and soon there were a couple of apartments on the top floor of the building where we lived. Come springtime, the building began to operate – albeit somewhat primitively – as a center for conferences, study, and retreat. Over the next few years, a number of families from local churches became an increasing part of the center's life, and it took on a life of its own.

There was something important and unusual about our upbringing at this point. We were being brought up as Christians in an entirely nondenominational or interdenominational setting, in which faith formed a key part of our lives, but not the ritual of institutional Christianity that we had been used to up to that time. It meant that we had to rub shoulders with people who had different points of view, and learn to assimilate the variety of perspectives that existed. Faith became something to be worked out in practice. It was about kindness and goodness, about seeing the needs of others as a part of your own human responsibility; it was about education and learning to understand others; it was about making life worth living. I grew up believing that although there was evil in the world people ultimately have the ability to be good.

And that was when we made our family visit to Israel, and a whole new chapter began to develop in our lives.

CHAPTER FOUR

Discovering the Jewish Tradition

When we returned from our holiday in Israel, life continued pretty much as it had before. Mother and Father worked very hard. James and I did our schoolwork and learned a lot about life from the comings and goings of the activities at Beth Shalom. As well as the conference work, people suffering from a range of personal problems would come and spend time at the center. They would be supported by my mother, whose energy and genuine compassion to look after people lost in the mire of human existence knew no bounds. No two days were the same, and so we experienced a life of color and variety. Of course, we lived "above the shop" and my parents did not draw a salary, so we never had anything but a very basic lifestyle and they worked twenty-four hours a day. They did what they did because they wanted to, and I discovered through their commitment that there is no greater reward than satisfaction at the outcome of one's labors. Through that day-in, day-out dedication to the cause of enriching human existence, I learned that to make the world a better place is an end in itself.

Our visit to Israel had sparked an informal interest in Israel as a country, but more broadly, in the Jewish tradition, history,

~~Never Again!~~ Yet Again!

religion, and culture. This didn't manifest itself in any particular way, except that we probably read a few more books, or watched a few more documentaries on the Jewish experience than would otherwise have been considered normal for the average Christian family living in the North Nottinghamshire coalfield. I remember shortly after our return borrowing Chaim Potok's *The Chosen*, *The Promise*, and *My Name Is Asher Lev*. Somehow, I had managed to switch from the amazing fantasy world of J.R.R. Tolkien's *Lord of the Rings* to issues of Jewish identity in late twentieth-century Lower East Side Manhattan. For some reason, I found the latter far more fascinating.

I am not quite sure why I chose to sit for religious studies in high school matriculation. Probably because I thought I could do it quite easily with my background, and also because Mother had been teaching it for years and had all the notes I would ever need. I took it a year earlier than my other examinations, along with English. I was momentarily proud of my achievement. I hadn't considered studying religious studies beyond this, as I only really wanted to add it to the tally at the end of my school career. I left school at sixteen. I had only one ambition – to be a farm manager! I had spent every vacation driving tractors since the age of thirteen. I had my own livestock business. I was sure that if I applied myself, I could become a farm manager.

I enjoyed starting work enormously, but needed more qualifications to progress. I decided to study for a bachelor's degree part-time and chose theology. I was already interested in the Jewish tradition and it seemed a good opportunity to further my knowledge more formally. The course was a Christian theology major. I pieced together my own minor route in Jewish studies, although there was no formal Jewish Studies department. I wanted to compare and contrast what I found, to get a sense of the underlying principles of the two religious traditions.

I found myself looking at two religious traditions that claimed many similarities in their origins, and yet seemed to have little, if anything, in common in belief or in practice. The deliberate creation of a set of differentiated feasts, fasts, and festivals began

Discovering the Jewish Tradition

to look a little as though Christianity had subversively carved out an identity for itself as far removed from its original source as possible. It seemed wrong to claim to inherit all of the prophecies and revelations from Jewish faith and history, and then to regard it as no longer viable. At this point, I was not gaining this understanding through classes, as it was not being taught. I was simply deducing that there appeared to be a huge tension in the relationship that was unhealthy. I found myself asking, "How is it that I am studying two religions emanating from the same traditional sources, in the same places and at the same time, and yet reading their respective histories, it is as if the two had never met?" It seemed that somewhere, the Christian world was not saying or admitting everything it should. In addition, it was clearly pushing Judaism out of the frame. I found this both disturbing and confusing. I was also becoming increasingly curious about the genesis of Christianity, and I began to suspect that the vast majority of Christians understood little of its origins and development. I simply wanted to know more.

I was an external student at London's Birkbeck College. I went down to London each year to do my exams. In the meantime, I worked with my parents. By this time, they had a mission developing churches and medical support in India. I spent many months there, swatting mosquitoes in the dark and learning to drive with one foot in the grave. Eventually, I came back to England at the age of nineteen and set up a couple of coffee shops in nearby towns, which occupied much of my time. Study came second, but I was determined that I wanted to know more about the complex relationship between Jews and Christians.

I carefully chose my topics of interest to cover as much of both Jewish and early Christian history as possible. For example, by studying "Early Israelite Religion" I found an obvious means of understanding something of the beginnings of the Jewish tradition. "Old Testament Studies" dealt with issues of Jewish identity, as I tried to understand the new and developing doctrines of an increasingly Roman Church. Studying the "Development of Jewish Literature" taught me about the codification of the oral

~~Never Again!~~ Yet Again!

tradition in the Talmud and its constituent consequence for Rabbinic Judaism. Finally, "Church History" was my way of evaluating how the Church, particularly in its early years, sought to form its own identity as distinct from Judaism. It was as close as I could get to a degree in Jewish Studies in a theology department that only offered one course with the word *Jewish* in the title. And my tutors and examiners never even knew!

Out of this experience, I began to encounter a very disturbing discovery – usually sitting late at night reading around the subject. As it dawned on me that the persecution of the Jews and the development of antisemitism were inseparably linked to the development and emergence of Christianity, I did not know what to do with this realization. Nobody was teaching me or coaching me through this, and at first I was somewhat scared by it. Its consequences were huge. If I were to admit it, maybe my own Christian identity would be shaken. I wondered if it would be a blasphemy of some kind. I found Rosemary Radford Ruether's book *Faith and Fratricide* in the library, and read it. I squirmed with concern and trepidation. Ruether describes in some detail the troubled relationship between Christianity and Judaism, and particularly the developing anti-Judaism, then the antisemitism of the emerging, then powerful Christian establishment. There was no one to signpost the next steps. I was confused. "What happens if this is not the case and she is deliberately making this out to despoil the Christian image?" That was the first thought to emanate from my disbelief at the treachery of Christianity toward Judaism. Surely it could not be true? Could it? Before I left the library, my question had changed. "And what if what she says is true?" That seemed worse.

It took me several months, personally and professionally, to come to terms with what I was learning. The more I read, the more it confirmed the fact that indeed Christians had first distanced themselves from the practices of Judaism through the persistence of anti-Judaism in their earliest teachings onward.

Christianity then appeared to have used its political, social, and economic power to isolate, discriminate against, and persecute Jews, simply because they were Jews, from the fourth century to the present day. I thought that this could not get any worse. Then I began to discover that I was also carrying the baggage of two thousand years of discrimination in the Western world. The language, the theology, the texts of Christianity in which I was immersed, with their persistent allusions to "new" as opposed to "old"; the use and abuse of texts within the Hebrew scriptures, which are used over and over again to justify the vilification of the Jews in the "messianic" era; and, perhaps worst of all, the reworking of the message and words of Jesus of Nazareth, himself a practicing Jew, in order to justify the removal of Christianity from the Jewish environment. The list was endless.

It was only at this point that I began to realize the importance of understanding and exploring the relationship between Jews and Christians in more detail. I decided to pursue my studies further and make it my concern to understand this relationship in the contemporary context.

Chapter Five
Jim and I

It sounds as if all these discoveries were being made and questions asked alone, but I am unintentionally misleading you somewhat. Throughout the years of inquiry and slow realization, it was a mutual, family interest, stemming from the first visit to Israel and the conversations that followed thereafter. Mother and I would discuss things because she was always interested. However, my closest ally and friend was – and is – my brother, James. You need to know about him, because without him this road of discovery would have been way too lonely to travel. We needed each other.

James is two years my junior; young enough to push around when you are eight, but old enough always to have been my closest friend. That is the way it always was. I pretend to make all the decisions, but really he was the one with all the opinions. It worked for us. We never fought. James was happy to have the opinions; I was happy to get things done.

While I was slowly working my way through my exams, he was already catching up on me, completing his medical degree just a year after I finished my undergraduate degree. This meant that intellectually we were coming of age at about the same time. The result was that we were able to spar on certain topics. As my medical knowledge was limited to high-school biology, I was not much fun on that front, and so we began to spend more time discussing, among other things, the issue of the Jewish-Christian relationship and the problem of antisemitism in the Christian

~~Never Again!~~ Yet Again!

tradition. James was studying in Leeds and I spent quite a lot of time at his house around exam times as I could gain access to libraries at Leeds University for cramming.

We began reading the British Jewish press and realized that we knew nothing much about the life of the Jewish community in Britain, and started to take a little more interest. Soon enough, we found a growing number of Jewish friends and our circle began to widen. We were taken to synagogue from time to time, attended lectures, and started to discover a world within a world. It was fascinating, absorbing, and interesting.

I began to wonder how to further my studies and how best to increase my knowledge of the Jewish-Christian relationship and its current dilemmas. I was looking for a topic that might make a suitable PhD subject and thought that spending some time learning about a Jewish community in contemporary British society would provide an insight into the community. I wanted to know more about its workings and the issues that face Jews today, aside from the Jewish-Christian issue. My intention at that point was to study the history and development of the Jews of Leeds.

James and I went one evening to listen to Professor Geoffrey Wigoder, formerly a Leeds man, who had become better known as editor in chief of the *Encyclopaedia Judaica* and a representative on the Catholic-Jewish Liaison Committee. Wigoder was speaking on the topic of "Jewish-Christian Relations since the Second World War," reflecting on what had happened in the relationship since the disaster of the Holocaust. His comments were enlightening and compelling, and demonstrated that the relationship still had much further to go. For some reason, his presence seemed too awesome for a direct approach that evening. Instead, I wrote to him in Jerusalem, explaining that it seemed there was much still to be done in this area (an understatement if there ever was one), and that James and I intended to dedicate some of our time and energies to engaging with this issue. His warm and encouraging response left us enthused to learn more.

In a bid to sound out the ground for my proposed thesis, I went to see Roy Graham, the *sheliach* – the Israel representative in

Jim and I

the community – in Leeds, who suggested that before I got any further involved in a study of the British Jewish community, I should spend some time in Israel. He pointed out that understanding Israel was important to an understanding of the British Jewish community. Not knowing quite what a *sheliach* was, I didn't know that he was bound to suggest such a course of action, but nevertheless James and I decided to spend the summer in Israel. I was awaiting my exam results and thought it an ideal opportunity to spend some time thinking about what to do next, meeting some people and learning some basic Hebrew. I signed up for the summer term at the Hebrew University. James, who had an elective period at university, chose to spend part of his time at Hadassah Hospital, at Ein Kerem, Jerusalem, and then a couple of weeks on the summer course. And so, in July 1991, we found ourselves back in Israel for what was to be another life-changing experience.

CHAPTER SIX
Confronting the Holocaust

While we were in Israel, James and I decided to use our spare time as fully as possible. We had a hunch that this would not be our last visit. We also knew that if work was to bring us back in the future, this was the time to see the sights and sounds of Israel. We went to the Israel Museum and to the Diaspora Museum in Tel Aviv. We walked the walls of the Old City of Jerusalem and David's Citadel. We walked the Mount of Olives and visited the Temple Mount. We went to the Knesset and even to the Jerusalem Zoo! Whatever Israel had to offer, we did it. However, there was one place that we wanted to visit that we considered an especially important undertaking. We decided we would not go as tourists, but with a personal obligation to face and to contemplate a particularly difficult part of the past. We made our way one hot July day to Yad Vashem, the Holocaust Martyrs' and Heroes' Remembrance Authority in Jerusalem.

We put the better part of a day aside to go there and try to understand a little more about the Holocaust, its history and meaning for the Jewish people. We already knew something about the Holocaust as our general interest in Jewish history had naturally attracted us to try to comprehend a little of what had happened. We had done the basic reading – Elie Wiesel's *Night*, Primo Levi's *The Drowned and the Saved*, *The Diary of Anne Frank*. We had watched the films, *Holocaust*, *Escape from Sobibor*, *Sophie's*

~~Never Again!~~ Yet Again!

Choice, even the full nine hours of Claude Lanzmann's *Shoah*. So we were not entirely new to the subject. We had absorbed some of the fundamental facts and figures and would have been able to hold a reasonably informed conversation about the Holocaust. In spite of this, we had never really stopped to ask ourselves what the Holocaust might mean for us as individuals. It was one of those things we thought we knew about, but actually had never taken the time or trouble to confront properly.

That day at Yad Vashem, we set out to try to understand the challenge of the Holocaust for us in a different way. We did not go there as Jews to confront a traumatic part of our identity, or knowing that had we been in Europe in the 1940s, we too would have been marked as victims of genocide. Nor were we there as the children of survivors whose whole lives had been turned upside down by the dark cloud of personal trauma and tragedy. We were not second-generation Germans who might have had to live with the guilt and anger of a previous generation's evil. We were just there as ourselves, largely detached and unaffected, asking what this might mean to us as individuals who could quite legitimately claim that it had nothing to do with us. Our question was, quite simply, "What is the challenge of the Holocaust for us?"

Walking around those darkened galleries had a profound and deeply troubling effect on me. It was not the faces or the actions of the perpetrators; it was not the scale of the camps or the efficiency of the system of death that the Nazis created, but rather the faces of the victims. I was less absorbed by what was done and how, but the people to whom it was done made no sense to me at all. And then the questions started to boil up. Why? Why did they do it? How could they do it? At times I was angry; at times I was sad, but most of all I was confused. It made absolutely no sense. Why would anyone want to take law-abiding, non-political, non-aggressive, innocent people and tear them apart, humiliate them, and then turn them to ashes? I stood in front of the well-known picture of the woman holding her baby as she was shot by a soldier from a few yards away. I turned to James and said, "That

Confronting the Holocaust

kid with the gun probably learned his history, his classics and his languages and graduated high school, then joined the army to serve his country, thinking it was a good cause. Look where he ended up. It's simply not all right to look at that and say, 'It's okay, we've moved on,' because clearly it is not okay. If it could happen then, what makes us so different?"

We emerged into the bright sunlight and sat in the beautifully landscaped memorial gardens, overlooking the valley below. We began asking questions of ourselves. Confronting the Holocaust at Yad Vashem is an intensely moving and emotional experience. It leaves one disoriented and in confused turmoil. There is the sense of loss and an overwhelming awareness of the evil that would create such destruction. The world was not the same place as we imagined just a couple of hours previously. But the overriding memory of that day is of the challenge it posed to us, as individuals, as professionals, and as part of the human race.

Our first question was, "Why the Jews?" We were coming into this with some background knowledge. We knew something of the richness of the tradition and culture of Jewish communities across Europe. We were well aware that they had led a harmless, poor, and often pious existence, with no interest in subverting the interests of any other group or society. The culture and contribution that Jews had been making to science and the arts for centuries was undeniable. Their tenacity in remaining a vital part of a largely hostile environment was as remarkable as it was productive. So why them?

Then there were questions around the roles of the perpetrators and bystanders. How was it that educated, civilized, cultured people could create such a monstrous state, in which the destruction of European Jewry could become such an integral aim? More troubling still was our concern that this was not just the ideological dream of a small clique of rabid antisemites. Every sector of German institutional and professional life had facilitated the aims of the Nazi regime and had consciously or subconsciously contributed to the success of the mass murder of the Jews of Europe. Individuals, too, had made choices daily to

~~Never Again!~~ Yet Again!

aid and abet the actions of the Nazis at all levels of society, and that included the persecution of many groups and individuals, as well as the genocide of the Jews.

We also thought about the mentality of evil that reduced the destruction of entire communities to a bureaucratic order. We now know from Heinrich Himmler's diaries that he was not just a bureaucrat behind a desk. We know that he traveled around the killing operations of Eastern Europe taking an avid interest in them. But behind Himmler was an army of people who were doing their jobs as they telegraphed the Eastern Front... and then Jewish children were murdered as a consequence. It's easy for me to say that they were all antisemites and therefore outcasts of the civilized world. It's more difficult to admit that they were human just like me; that they did their PhDs, played the piano, visited the opera and enjoyed their skiing in the Alps; that they went to church, said their prayers and told their children to be good. These people learned to heal, to invent, and to communicate. They created laws, took pride in their education and dreamed of a perfect future. But the question for us that day was, "At what cost?"

As we extended our discussion, we found ourselves asking questions about the professions. Judges, who were trained to dispatch justice, sent people to forced labor or to their deaths because of who they happened to be, or what they happened to believe. Teachers stood in front of their classes and taught race sciences and political propaganda week after week, many of them knowing that the "knowledge" they bestowed upon their pupils was spurious and dangerous. Doctors, trained to heal the body and the mind, carried out the T4-euthanasia program and sterilized tens of thousands of "socially unacceptable" individuals. It was medical professionals who carried out the selections on the ramp at Birkenau and medical professionals who took "research opportunities," experimenting on otherwise perfectly healthy individuals, killing them, or maiming them for life. Clergy, charged with the Christian message of hope, forgiveness, love, and goodness, incited their congregations to hatred or allowed them the liberty or passivity, and hence the guilt, of collusion.

Confronting the Holocaust

Did they know? Of course they did. But very often, what you say you know is limited by what you are prepared to admit. Stunned by the realization that this happened in the real world of real people, James and I began to ask whether our society had really confronted this stark reality. We sat on one of the benches along the Avenue of the Righteous and asked, "If, God forbid, we were given a second chance, how would we do next time? Have we learned anything? Have we progressed at all?"

We were aware that the Holocaust had been marginalized and that its most prominent feature was an uneasy silence. We also somehow knew that there were some signs in British society that the Holocaust was being confronted. At that time, the War Crimes Bill was taking a very protracted and convoluted route through the legislature. The fact that Britain was considering the prosecution of Nazi war criminals at all was interesting, even if there appeared to be only a slim chance of securing convictions. The determination to put on record that such crimes should not go unpunished was as important to Britain as any trials that might follow. The House of Commons was passing the bill; the House of Lords rejected it. The War Crimes Bill became a moral and legal ping-pong ball, traveling back and forth between the Houses. Eventually, Margaret Thatcher invoked the little-used Parliament Act to force the bill onto the statute books. It was clear from this process that some sectors of British society wanted to avoid a confrontation with the Nazi past, or even to cover it up.

At the same time, there had been discussion about study of the Holocaust becoming part of the new national curriculum for England and Wales. Greville Janner MP was vociferously campaigning both for the War Crimes Bill and the inclusion of the Holocaust on the national curriculum, and he had started the Holocaust Educational Trust to lobby on behalf of these issues. As a result, "The Holocaust" was soon to be listed as a compulsory topic on the history curriculum for students in Key Stage 3 (11–14-year-olds). So progress was being made behind the scenes, although James and I were not aware of the details when we stood at Yad Vashem that day.

~~Never Again!~~ Yet Again!

We did know that there were areas where the Holocaust was not being addressed at all. As a medical student, James had just completed an introductory course in medical ethics. We could not understand how such a course, even taking into account its brevity, could not at least reference the Holocaust as a warning from medical history. If the aim of such a course is to question the boundaries of modern medicine, and within that the role of personal and professional choices, surely some sense of what can go wrong would be instructive? The medical students of Berlin and Vienna of the 1920s did not train to maim, murder, and kill. And yet some of these graduates went on to do just that. Some 45 percent of the medical profession were voluntary members of the Nazi Physicians' League. Not all took part directly in harming human life. However, they did associate themselves with a regime that ultimately committed genocide in their name, as its members. Matters of choice are important. To serve one's career or an ideology of any kind at the expense of the life or dignity of any individual is to abandon the very cause of medicine. James commented that "Education is important at that level because if it did happen, it shows it can, and therefore it might… Is that not warning enough?"

I came from an entirely different field of study. As a graduate theologian, I was concerned about my total lack of understanding of the role of the Christian Churches in the success of National Socialism, and by extension in the mass destruction of European Jewry. The persistence of antisemitism within the Christian tradition and the connivance of Christianity with National Socialism seemed too coincidental to be ignored. I was wondering why nobody had told me that in July 1933 both Protestant and Catholic Churches had committed themselves to institutional relationships that tied them to the framework of the National Socialist state. They did not desist in that relationship for the full twelve years of Nazi domination. Of course, there were a few lonely voices of dissent. But they were not speaking on behalf of the Church, but rather in spite of it. "Where does that leave the Christian Church?" I found myself asking. "Did the Churches preserve their institutional survival at the expense of their moral and spiritual credibility? Can Christianity still claim to have any credibility after such an unforgivable desertion of its 'Christian' cause within society?"

We were still sitting on the Avenue of the Righteous at Yad Vashem. Thousands of non-Jewish individuals are remembered there for what they did in saving Jewish lives from otherwise certain death. There is no doubt that these were real heroes who defied the full force of National Socialism and took on the Nazis single-handedly. Of course, they never would – and never could – defeat them alone. But that is not why they took action. They acted because they felt they could. Many times subsequently, I have been asked, "Why were there so few who were 'Righteous among the Nations'?" There are currently over 26,000 people who have been recognized by the State of Israel for their outstanding courage. For a while, I tried to answer that question – until one day I realized it was the wrong question altogether. There were indeed relatively few who acted with such courage, but it seems you can only really ask that question if you are absolutely certain that you would be one of them. If you can say for certain that you would risk your life, that of your spouse and children, and everything you have and own, to help a complete stranger to whom you owe absolutely nothing, then you can ask that question: Why weren't there more? If you do not know for certain that you could do that, then the question has to be: How were there so many prepared to take a risk I am not sure I could take myself? The fact that the Avenue of the Righteous runs right through the heart of Yad Vashem is valuable, because the people recognized there are the answer to the dilemma of silence, compliance, and collaboration. They showed very clearly that there was another way.

At the end of our visit to Yad Vashem, James and I decided that we must respond in some practical way to what we had seen. It did not feel right to walk away from there and carry on with our normal lives as if nothing of consequence had happened. The Holocaust, it appeared, actually had huge consequences for us

~~Never Again!~~ Yet Again!

and for our generation. People have often asked us since, "How is it that millions of individuals go to Yad Vashem and are moved by what they see there, but very few react in the way that you did?" The answer does not lie in our reaction to the atrocities, but in the feeling of being let down. Let down by Western civilization, by our teachers, our mentors, our society, by all those who failed to raise the Holocaust with us. It was self-apparent that the Holocaust was an issue with which we should engage, and yet we knew that most of our peers would be totally disengaged from it. As an event in human history, the Holocaust also flew directly in the face of the value system we had been brought up with; it railed against us in the most forceful of ways. Somehow we simply could not allow it to be ignored. It seemed too important for that.

We felt let down by the education system in particular. We wanted to know how it was possible to go through school and university, and even to take an interest in Jewish history and culture, without anyone at any point in our formal education saying to us, "Listen, this is the Holocaust; it is a tragedy of immense proportions for the Jewish community, but it also matters to you." Although we knew something of the history of the Holocaust, we were in our mid-twenties and just discovering and confronting it for the first time as an issue that raised significant challenges for our own lives. Suddenly, we were faced with huge questions, but apparently nobody was armed with any answers. The propensity of otherwise good people to be extraordinarily evil; the nature of responsibility in society; the choices one makes, and the impact these have on the lives of others; the strength and weakness of democracy; and the importance of valuing human life: these and many other issues bombarded us.

On the other hand, our reaction was also conditioned by the shattering of an idealistic belief in human goodness, in spite of the evil and suffering in the world. Until that point, we had believed that good would ultimately prevail, or at least pull through in the end. During the Holocaust, evil had triumphed and there appeared to be very little goodness. It turned our moral

Confronting the Holocaust

world upside down. Instead of hope, there was despair; instead of goodness, there was evil. Try as we might, there seemed little to commend any optimism in human endeavor and behavior. Clearly, the propensity for wanton destruction was deeply embedded in Western civilization – and, we suspected, in any civilization for that matter.

I consider myself to be a creative person. The appreciation of beautiful things, and in particular the immense beauty of the natural world, is part of my enjoyment of life. My hobbies as a youngster were music, photography, writing, and travel – the sorts of activities that allowed me to engage in creating, communicating, and appreciating the world in which I found myself. My reaction to the Holocaust was never motivated by morbid fascination, but rather by a distinct revulsion at the destruction of peace-loving, ordinary, yet beautiful people. It ran counter to the things that inspire me and uplift me, make me believe in life. I therefore wanted to confront it. It angered me, it saddened me, and it strengthened my resolve. Confronting the Holocaust meant finding ways of creating beauty for the future, in spite of the ugliness of the past. I wanted to find out what had allowed the Holocaust to occur and begin to confront it, because without such a confrontation, repetition was more likely – or at least so it appeared. On one level, becoming absorbed with the Holocaust was something I didn't want to do. That is, I had no inclination to do so for its own sake. Knowing which camp was run by which commandant, on what budget, decided by which policy, was less important to me than establishing the broad principles that lay behind the catastrophe. Most importantly, I became involved because the Holocaust represented the opposite of everything I believed human societies should be.

And so the questions kept coming. "What does it tell us about human nature?" "Are we likely to repeat this kind of behavior?" "Where does this leave our ethics, politics, and economics?" "Where does this leave the business community when businesses made prudent 'commercial decisions' and invested in their corporate future in the Third Reich?" "Were the thousands who

~~Never Again!~~ Yet Again!

were enslaved and worked to death a mere incidental outcome to this?" The terror of enslavement and persecution did not square with what we thought we knew about the values of an educated civilization. It seemed incomprehensible to think that this was not the Egypt of four millennia ago, but Europe in the twentieth century.

We knew that the Holocaust was a tragedy of immense proportions for the Jewish community, the effects of which would take several generations to be realized. But we discovered something at Yad Vashem that day that we did not expect to encounter quite so strongly. For the first time, we understood that the Holocaust is not a Jewish "problem" at all. Somehow I had previously come to accept the fact that the Holocaust was an issue dealt with by Jews. As I understood it, Jewish people had generally contributed to making the films, books, and documentaries I had seen or read. Clearly, it is important that members of the Jewish community document and represent this, as it is indeed the most painful chapter of a very painful past. But our question was, "Where is everybody else?" Surely, Jews did not perpetuate antisemitism or perpetrate mass death; they suffered the consequences of antisemitism and the genocidal policies of others. Therefore the "problem" whatever it was, seemed to lie fairly and squarely outside the Jewish community and was ingrained in Western European civilization somewhere. And so the responsibility to address and confront it also needs to be taken up by a broad spectrum of people prepared to make that cause their own. As we sat there in the heat of the Israeli summer, among the mêlée of questions we were asking, one kept coming back: "Why has no one done anything about this?"

We knew that across Europe there were already a few physical or educational spaces that offered a meaningful response to the tragedy and challenge of the Holocaust. Former Nazi-occupied territories have hundreds of sites of destruction containing memorials of some kind, but we suspected that they were there by default rather than design. They were being maintained because they had to be, rather than because European society was taking

Confronting the Holocaust

the issue of the Holocaust seriously. In some ways, these sites had become an excuse not to deal with the Holocaust, as they were an unfortunate *fait accompli* on the landscape of European memory. What we were looking for was a response that demonstrated real care, rather than begrudging duty. If all that happened was a preservation program for decaying sites, a number of road signs and clusters of guides who could tell you about the history, development, and mechanics of the camps, what would that contribute to an examination of European society in the wake of its darkest hour?

In particular, we were concerned about the ignorance of the British public who seemed to suffer from what we saw as some kind of "victor's syndrome." Britain played a crucial role as a member of the Allied Forces – along with the Americans in particular – who took on the might of the German army and ultimately crushed and punished them and restored democracy. But perhaps because of that final success, it appeared that we in Britain no longer felt the need to address the Holocaust as a cause for concern. It had not happened in Britain. Perhaps we felt a sense of moral high ground in which "that" debacle was "their" doing – that of the Nazis, with whom we had long disassociated and fought. The Second World War is a heroic memory of struggle and determination against the odds in Britain. For those who risked their lives and gave their lives, it should be. It took much heartache and not a little commitment to make possible the ultimate defeat of Nazism, and it was service of immense importance. Still today, the legends of the Battle of Britain, D-Day, and ultimately VE-Day make an Englishman's heart throb. Say "Dig for Victory" and everyone knows exactly what you mean. However, if you were to refer to *Nacht und Nebel, Einsatzgruppen, Judenrat, die Endlösung, die Judenfrage,* and *Aktion,* the frightening terminology of Nazi genocidal occupation, the average Briton would look at you blankly.

There are reasons for this, of course. There was the Cold War, with a Soviet threat which meant that British sensitivities toward its German adversaries had to be quickly turned into a relation-

~~Never Again!~~ Yet Again!

ship of constructive partnership, in which addressing the Holocaust was not helpful. Britain's position in Palestine and its relationship with the new state of Israel did not readily foster sympathy with Jewish suffering, as it was perceived to give too much leverage to Palestinian Jews in pursuit of their independence. And so, somehow, the Holocaust was all but ignored in Britain for a very long time.

James and I felt that it was vitally important for British society to be confronted with the meaning and challenge of the Holocaust, and that as a society we should ask ourselves what kind of issues we should be addressing, in order to be more certain that future generations are better informed than our own. As we left Yad Vashem that day, we decided to dedicate some of our time, energy, and resources to assisting the British public in confronting the Holocaust and evaluating something of its meaning for their lives. We thought we might volunteer for an organization or spend some time encouraging European governments to consider ways to engage the wider public in confronting the Holocaust. We just knew we wanted to do something and determined to go about it on our return to England.

That evening, we arrived back at our temporary home – our room at the Hebrew University on Har HaTsofim, Jerusalem – and were invited out by a couple who had become friends on the summer course. They were a very pleasant, amiable pair whose friendship was not hard to cultivate. He was Dutch and his wife German. As we sat in their apartment, eating supper, we explained that we had been at Yad Vashem that day. We told them how moved we had been and how much we wanted to find a way to respond to what we had seen there. In passing, I asked whether they had been to Yad Vashem yet. To my surprise, the young woman replied in very negative tones that she had been to school in Germany; that she had done "that history" year after year and did "not intend to do it again." I was taken aback, possibly even insulted by the way in which she responded to something that was challenging the fundamentals of my very existence that day. (Since that first encounter with German young people

Confronting the Holocaust

overloaded on Holocaust history, I have come to be more sympathetic. I now understand that the way in which Holocaust history was taught in Germany for many years was more likely to create barriers and resistance than to encourage openness and confrontation, a situation which has significantly changed in many instances in Germany today.) My reaction to this was to become even more determined to try to make people understand that this is not just *another* history, nor one that we should be afraid to encounter. It is one we must be prepared to confront in all its troubling reality.

There is something about the way people react to other people that very often affects the way things work out. The people we met played a major role in the way we developed our ideas. They were the push and pull of each phase we went through. Some people were very supportive and helpful, giving timely words of advice or encouragement. A few were disparaging or disbelieving. Either way, we checked our conscience against their views and learned from whatever they had to say. We did find ready listeners in our parents, who had come over to Israel for a short holiday during our stay there. We explained what we had experienced at Yad Vashem and our concerns about apathy towards the Holocaust among many members of the British public. We discussed the need to raise this with our peers, and particularly with a Christian world which we perceived as still largely indifferent to the challenges posed by the Holocaust. We did not know quite what form such an undertaking should take, and were certainly not thinking of doing anything ourselves.

The next day, we found ourselves discussing all this with an Israeli taxi driver, Yossi Turgeman. Although the task of bringing this challenge to the wider public seemed somewhat daunting, Yossi's obvious enthusiasm and his view that such things should, and could, be undertaken by non-Jews, was our first indication that this was a history we could share in for the sake of our joint future. He does not know it, but the opportunity to share our concern with someone else who was prepared to listen marked the very first step on our way.

~~Never Again!~~ Yet Again!

It had been my practice since my early teens, whenever I found something meaningful, to try to write it down in poetry or find ways of expressing it in music. On returning from Yad Vashem, I created a series of poems and musical pieces to capture my reaction at the time. In those pieces I struggled with the broad issues of life and death, with responsibility, suffering, and loss. I reflected on the callousness of the perpetrators and the dilemmas of the victims. It all came out in a flood of contemplation that spun around my head for weeks on end. Looking back, I am pleased I did that. Although I would not necessarily write the same pieces now, I know that the response I formulated at the time was heartfelt. It seems important to me that any response to human tragedy should be made in as human a way as possible. That means thinking personally and empathetically about the consequences for those caught up in it. It means putting yourself into their shoes and grappling with the dangers, struggling with the consequences. To respond to such a tragedy as an intellectual exercise is not enough, and indeed is arguably inappropriate if it is the only response. On the other hand, simply to react emotionally, without facing the inherent intellectual, political, societal challenge it poses, is to escape its consequences. What I was trying to do was respond appropriately, by feeling the immense human tragedy and finding the right way to be challenged by it. And the challenge turned out to be bigger than I had ever imagined possible.

Among the many reflections of that time I wrote "My Little Light," lyrics to a song dedicated to the children of the ghettos. I guess it was the realization that children were a specific target of the Nazis as they represented the future and continuity, which was profoundly shocking. I tried to process that. I still do. It is a reflection that continues to have meaning for me, especially as I am a parent now.

My Little Light

My little light
You've shone through the darkness
You've shone through the blackness of the night
Don't cry my child,
Your light is still burning,
I haven't forgotten
Little flickering flame

When you stood on the ghetto corner,
Older than your years
So brave in the face of danger
You were just a child,
Holding back those tears

And when I look at your lonely faces,
When I see your eyes
I know your hearts were asking,
When can I be free?
Mama, who am I?

My little light
You've shone through the darkness
You've shone through the blackness of the night
Don't cry my child,
Your light is still burning,
I haven't forgotten,
Little flickering flame.

Chapter Seven
Where Memories Meet

I was talking to one or two Holocaust survivors, explaining the interest James and I had in the Holocaust and that we really wanted to know more. They were very encouraging and suggested I keep learning. One of them was Ben Helfgott, founder of the '45 Aid Society, more affectionately known as "The Boys," as documented by Martin Gilbert. Ben suggested that before going much further, we should take a trip to Poland to see what had happened there, to whom, where, and how. He said, "Stephen, when I go to Poland, it is like a large Jewish cemetery. I know where my mother was murdered, and I know where my sister was murdered, because they were locked in the synagogue for two weeks before they were taken out and shot. But as for everyone else in my family and in my community, Poland was turned into a factory of death. You should see this to understand it." In January 1992, my parents, James, and I took the car and made our way to Poland.

Our route was not direct, though. We started in Germany, driving down to Munich, where we spent the day, and also to Nuremberg. We then traveled on to Prague where we visited the Jewish quarter and cemetery and, of course the Altneu Shul. The impression of those cobbled streets, old houses of prayer and the thousands of lonely graves will remain etched in my memory. It was that sense of Jewish life where there is no Jewish life. It was

~~Never Again!~~ Yet Again!

not what we saw, but what was missing that most embedded itself in my conscience. At the time, they were just beginning to paint the names of the deportees on the wall of the Pinkas Synagogue, where now 80,000 names of Jews of Bohemia and Moravia are permanently inscribed. A young woman sat atop the scaffolding, painstakingly painting one name after another. It seemed tedious, until I reminded myself that every name was a life – and that in most cases, that one moment of inscription would be the only memorial they would ever have. Each name was like a funeral, fifty years late.

From there we headed into southern Poland and on to Krakow. The fact that the majority of the Jewish population was wiped out during its Nazi occupation, and that hundreds of thousands of Jews were brought there from right across the European continent for the sole purpose of killing them, makes it a place of very great tragedy in the whole of human history. However, we quickly discovered that Poland is not a Jewish cemetery at all.

I remember standing at the end of the ramp at Birkenau, where some one million Jewish men, women, and children had been unloaded before they were murdered, and realizing that although this was their final resting place, it was hardly a cemetery. At a cemetery you see the individual graves of individual people. There are names, dates of birth and death, and each has a headstone bearing some personal symbol or epitaph in honor of that loved one. In a cemetery there is ritual; there is family and community; there is dignity and love. As I looked around me in the silence, I imagined the tired and dirty deportees arriving at this, their final destination. Within hours of arriving, they were stripped, gassed, and burned, and everything they had brought with them was looted by their murderers. I went through the Jewish rites of death and mourning in my mind and soon realized that every rite, as practiced in the Jewish religion, had been desecrated there. Ben was right, though. Death and absence were everywhere. I only understood what he meant when I saw it for myself.

Where Memories Meet

Although in life many of us do not associate so closely with our respective religious communities, in death we are buried by our co-religionists. Then we are laid to rest alongside them as part of that community and its history. Whether the individuals who had ended their lives at Birkenau were religious or secular, the vast majority would ordinarily have been buried according to Jewish tradition in Jewish cemeteries. I looked around me. "Where are the *matzevot* – the headstones? Where are the names, the dates of birth and of death? Where are the individuals, the families, the communities, the dignity and love for the deceased?" They were not there.

The next day, we spent some time traveling around the Polish countryside, and en route we passed through many small towns and former *shtetlach* – villages. We knew that before the war Jews represented over ten percent of the Polish population and our guidebook told us something about the Jewish communities that had existed in the region. It didn't take long to realize that in each of those towns and villages there was no visible Jewish presence of any kind. The synagogues are gone – or perform another secular function. The Jewish schools are gone too, and the *yeshivot*, the schools of Talmudic learning, along with the *mikvaot*, the ritual baths, the kosher bakers and butchers, the youth movements, the Communists and the labor Zionists. All are gone and will never return. The last remnants of these once thriving communities are found in the disheveled, unkempt, and at times vandalized cemeteries scattered across the countryside. We were looking for something that was no longer there. We were looking for people who had gone.

This fact was even more profoundly impressed upon me on a subsequent trip to Belzec. It was towards the end of winter; some two feet of snow lay on the ground and had been building up over about a two-week period. I was going to Belzec because I knew that over 600,000 Jews had been murdered there. I was not ready, however, for the "memorial" I was to find: a small, untidy piece of scrubland with a fence that had clearly not been maintained, and a square concrete monument that managed to avoid informing

~~Never Again!~~ Yet Again!

visitors that the victims of Belzec were Jews. What struck me most of all when we arrived was that although there were two feet of snow, not so much as a single set of footprints was to be found in it. No one had even entered that site for over two weeks.

Today the scene at Belzec is very different. A field of clinker covers the hillside, which is cut through with a walkway, a tunnel through ashes which leads to the heart of where the gas chambers were. It is a profound and telling memorial, demanding questions, defying answers. But that day, at the deserted and forgotten Belzec, I realized that the Holocaust was not only about the mass murder of European Jewry, but it was also an attempt to wipe out even the memory of the existence of those individuals and communities. On that day, I realized just how successful the Holocaust had been. I had always consoled myself with the fact that it was not total, that the Jewish community had managed to revive itself, that lessons had been learned, that Israel now existed, and the Jews had rediscovered their identity around the world and a future could be built. That day, I realized that what happened was entirely a waste of life. I realized that absolutely nothing good comes out of the Holocaust. If anything is salvaged, it is not because of the Holocaust, but in spite of it. This turned upside down a principle that I had held, that out of bad things good can come – the kind of naïve optimism that because the Nazis were defeated and the Jews live on, that in some way there was "victory." But it is a very hollow victory indeed. Out of bad things, bad things come. Anything good that emerges merely helps us to make sense of living, but does not reverse the effect of the evil or undo the damage. The Holocaust was a waste of life; it was the desecration of life, the trampling of life, the humiliation, degradation, wanton destruction of people for meaningless power and nothing else. What sense was there in taking a child and shooting him through the heart? What sense was there in taking a man and wearing him down with fear every day until he was thrown into the abyss? Or in taking a mother and destroying her in front of her children? Or even worse, in destroying the children in front of the mother? It was taking the dignified and

Where Memories Meet

turning them into animals. There is nothing, absolutely nothing, good about any of that.

It was then that I knew for certain that far more is lost than can ever be recovered. Among those hundreds of thousands of people were talents and skills, homes and institutions, learning and creativity – and it all lay in a heap under the soil beneath my feet, either unrealized or destroyed in the carnage. I understood that far more is forgotten than can ever be retained or remembered. Belzec is arguably one of the most significant historical sites anywhere on the European continent. Since my first visit there, the estimated number of victims of Belzec has risen from 600,000 to as many as 800,000. All were murdered in the space of ten months in 1942. At the time, there was no indication at the memorial of who those people were, where they came from, or what family they left behind – if any at all. There was just a space where their anonymous remains were scattered. Only two people are said to have survived Belzec. The tragedy of this is that hardly a single member of the general public could identify that Belzec was linked to the Holocaust, let alone tell you what happened there. It is arguably one of the most significant sites in human history, as it was there that Christian Wirth perfected the method of killing human beings en masse using poisonous gas, before using it very effectively to destroy in excess of three quarters of a million people on a fifteen-acre site. Auschwitz became the icon, Treblinka became a symbol, but Belzec was the real deal. It was secret, effective, unknown, and forgotten – just as the Nazis intended.

On another occasion, I had the privilege to be in Poland for two weeks with Dr. Jonathan Webber, then of Oxford University, who was running a European Union Tempus program, bringing together English, German, and Polish students to confront the Holocaust, its history, and consequences. This was also a seminal experience, not least because the mix of students was such that simply being able to talk together about the Holocaust in a meaningful way revealed just how differently we perceived this history. The same history that took place in the same places had an

~~Never Again!~~ Yet Again!

entirely different meaning to each of those on the trip. For some, it was painful and personal; for others, distant and less important. In talking to the participants, I began to realize that there is not a single version of the Holocaust. We all overlay it with our own interpretations and contexts. The key thing I learned was that I would always need to be careful not to read this history in the way that suited me, but always to listen to what others had to say.

The most important part of the visit was spending a whole week in the towns, villages, cemeteries, and synagogues of once-thriving communities, and beginning to understand further just how much had been destroyed. Jonathan took us to Tarnow, to Nowy Sacz, and to Bobowa, as well as to a host of little places with long and significant Jewish histories. It was powerful and engaging to touch so much Jewish culture in such a short space of time. The void of absence in those towns was yawning, a chasm of emptiness waiting to be filled. Jonathan had an amazing ability to be able to find and explain in detail old synagogues, cemeteries, inscriptions on walls, *mezuzot* in doorways, former *sukkot* from the Feast of Tabernacles, clinging to rooftops fifty years later. At Dabrowa Tarnowska, I remember wandering around the grand old crumbling synagogue, its mural of the Twelve Tribes of Israel faded but still merged into broken plaster which was about to peel from the rotting walls. In that town, the community had been large enough, proud enough to develop that wonderful building. They had designed it, built it, painted it, prayed in it. And now it was empty, a relic of a vanished civilization. Its scale spoke volumes. It was not a small building tucked behind a grocer's store; it was huge, central, and cavernous. Whoever lived there was immensely proud of their tradition. It was a major landmark in the town. We wandered around the corner to the cemetery, where we were met by the last surviving Jew of the community there. To my shame, I don't even remember his name, but I recollect so clearly standing watching as he talked, realizing that when this old man was gone, there really would be nothing except the disintegrating synagogue.

Where Memories Meet

I saw more clearly how our representations of the past can either reveal or conceal. These forgotten places of the Holocaust were concealed by layers of amnesia, which heap insult on its injury. Over the week we were there, we hardly ventured more than an hour or two away from Krakow. Yet day after day, we picked among the ruins of destruction and saw only the shadows of a former world. When I looked at the small area of the map we had covered, calculating just how much destruction we had seen and how little was left, then scanned the whole of the European continent where the result had been so similar in so many places, it became even harder to comprehend. My hopes that I would begin to understand this trauma were becoming less and less likely with everything I saw and learned.

I also encountered the despair of the Holocaust in a different way. We went to visit Tarnow town, about an hour's drive from Krakow. There was formerly a ghetto in Tarnow and one of the first transports to Auschwitz went from the town, which included Jews and Poles rounded up and put into some of the first labor battalions there. A few kilometers outside the town lies a small hamlet called Zbylitowska Gora. The ghetto in Tarnow was quite substantial. In 1942 it housed some 40,000 Jewish people. One day, approximately 6,000 Jews were taken from the ghetto, marched the several kilometers to Zbylitowska Gora and murdered in a small woodland on June 11, 1942. The beauty mixed with anguish there was quite overwhelming. The trees were majestic and quiet, allowing sunlight to filter down to the mass graves below their towering canopy. There was a low fence approximately demarcating the positions of the graves. On one of them, there was a plaque dedicated to the 800 Jewish children murdered there that day. This left me in a blinding despair I will never forget. "How could such innocent life be wasted? Who were those children? Does anyone know? Does anyone care?" The wasted lives of 800 children of Zbylitowska Gora were helping me make sense both of the scale and intimacy of death in a way that neither Birkenau nor Belzec could. In those places of such huge scale, people are very quickly consumed by statistics

~~Never Again!~~ Yet Again!

and symbolism. It is hard to struggle against the tide of mass death, because the whole intent was to depersonalize and obfuscate the victims through the sheer numbers of their victimhood. At Zbylitowska Gora, I knew I was looking at the grave of the generation of Tarnow's Jews who should be leading the community now. They would be the grandparents of today, but were buried in a hole of yesterday's madness. The children buried in front of me would have been around the same age as my parents. Their lives had been utterly wasted because of who they were. As the numbers became smaller and the communities that had once existed came more and more into focus, I was now beginning to realize what the real consequences of the Holocaust were. This didn't make things any easier to understand, but knowing just how much there was to know began to give a greater sense of direction to our own endeavors.

We also visited a Jewish cemetery in Nowy Sacz. In the middle of the largely deserted landscape, there is a small *ohel* – a small mausoleum over the grave of a righteous person. In the *ohel* two members of the Halberstam Hasidic dynasty are buried. The *tzadikim*, the righteous people buried there, would long since have been forgotten if members of their family and followers had not emigrated before the Nazi occupation. Today, their followers make the journey back to Nowy Sacz to remember their founders. It was sunset when we arrived there and in the half light of the *ohel*, as we peered in, we could see a little *yahrzeit* candle, a memorial candle, flickering in the darkness. It was apparent that someone had made the journey there to remember the *rebbe*, because his life, teaching, and wisdom still had meaning in their lives today. His followers would light their candle, say their prayers and return to their homes, wherever they may be. I thought about the forgotten victims of Belzec and the anonymous children of Zbylitowska Gora, and realized that no one visited them because they were forgotten, without a name or an identity to remember them by. It became clear to me that it is the duty of anyone – or perhaps everyone – to make time to reflect and remember them, because we are the only memory they have.

Where Memories Meet

On returning home to England, I couldn't see through the pain of the loss. I couldn't escape the screams that must have punctured streets and houses, synagogues and barracks alike. Nor could I escape the silence; the silence of inner anguish, of inevitability, of knowing and not admitting; the silence of empty space, of relics, of mass graves; the silence of not listening, not speaking, not responding; the silence of silence, the noise of silencing, the silence of the pleading victims. I couldn't get out of my head that the world had been broken, shattered by the Holocaust. It was a breakage of such force that I was certain it could never be mended.

And in the silence, the scream became ever louder in my head.

Above: Beth Shalom, 1978
Right: Jim and me together in Israel, 1991
Below: Visiting Yad Vashem, 1991

Mother, Jim, and me together in Israel, 1991

Construction work begins in the gardens at the Centre as I come to grips with driving the JCB, 1992

Above: The memorial hall under construction, 1992

Left: The roof goes on, 1993

Below: A maturing garden surrounds the finished memorial hall, 1998

Main Photo: Beth Shalom, seen through the main entrance gates
Inset: The Gateway of the Righteous, set in the memorial gardens

The memorial garden: a place of peace in spite of the suffering it represents

The memorial rose gardens, a significant and poignant part of the Centre, where many people have planted roses for lost families, alongside those dedicated by school groups and civic dignitaries

Left: Jewish refugee Lisa Vincent talks with students in the hall at the Centre

Below: James fits an image in the Camp Room of the exhibition

Bottom: In the memorial exhibition; more than just photos and suitcases, these provide a means to visualize the environments described

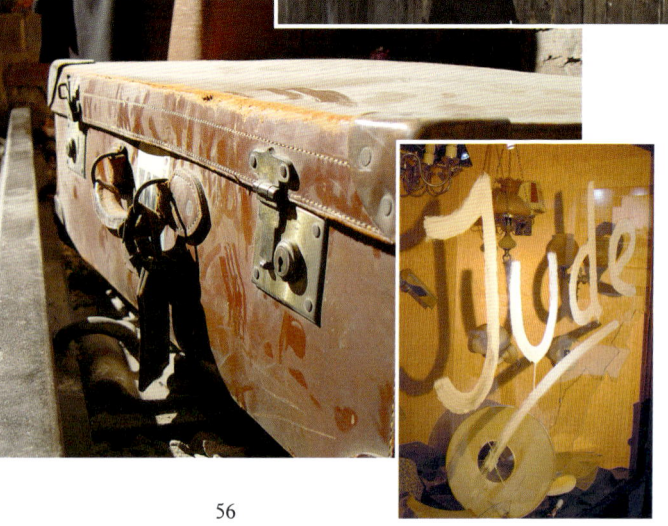

Abandoned: *A sculpture by survivor Naomi Blake*

Above: Members of a group relaxing on the patio over tea

Left: Mother with her customary greeting

Right: Professor Yehuda Bauer, then research director at Yad Vashem, delivers a keynote lecture in the memorial hall, September 1997

Below: School pupils listening to a survivor relating his experiences in the memorial hall

PART TWO
DECISIONS

PART TWO – DECISIONS
CHAPTER EIGHT
MAKING MEMORY

James and I decided that whatever we were going to do in response to our learning about the Holocaust, it should be done foremost in remembrance of those who were forgotten. We felt that the struggle against amnesia, obfuscation, and denial was the most important thing to engage in first of all. But still we had no real idea about how to go about this. Clearly, we were in no position to name the victims of Belzec or Zbylitowska Gora or the hundreds of other sites strewn around the European landscape. We felt there ought to be some kind of memorial space and began to wonder, "What kind of place should exist? Where? To say what? Run by whom? And toward what end?" None of this was abundantly clear, other than the fact that someone should do something – and soon.

In the meantime, I had taken a year off, prior to starting my doctoral thesis. I wanted to find a topic I felt more comfortable with, and also to spend some additional time doing further fundamental learning in Jewish studies. I spent a year at the Oxford Centre for Hebrew and Jewish Studies with Professor David Patterson on the one-year graduate program. This turned out to be an important year for many reasons. Not only did I have all the hours of the day for reading and attending courses on subjects I loved, but I also found the time to think and reflect more.

One Sunday evening, traveling back to Oxford from home, I was becoming a little frustrated. It was clear that what was needed was some kind of museum, memorial, and education

~~Never Again!~~ Yet Again!

center in the UK, a place that could confront British society with its own negligence and pose important questions which until that time were still studiously avoided. I was thinking about how a site might be found and the government persuaded to assist in funding such a project, how much it might cost, and where the team would come from to create it. More importantly, I wondered where several million pounds might come from to buy a site, construct a building, and service an institution in London. It became apparent as I thought it through that it was not going to happen. Not then, anyway.

Time was passing by and it seemed that such a project could not wait forever. At the same time, a memorial to the Holocaust needed to be set in a place worthy of its purpose. It should be a place of reflection and dignity, a place for learning and confrontation with the past. I then realized that we were expecting everybody else to do something about this; now I asked what were we ourselves prepared to do? As if someone had turned on the light, everything became very clear. Beth Shalom, the retreat my parents were running, was the obvious place to do something. I couldn't wait to talk to James and, of course, we would have to sit down and talk with our parents too since they owned the building!

The initial idea was very modest. We talked it through together and felt that a project on the Holocaust, with a number of rooms for a library and some pictures on a wall to serve as some kind of exhibit, would probably be the best we could manage. At least that way we could ensure that visitors to the Centre, and local schools and universities, would have the opportunity to come and be confronted by a small but meaningful place, and discuss their reactions to it. It would mean that we would be making some kind of contribution, rather than worrying about the fact that nothing was available in the UK.

It soon became clear, however, that a room with a few Holocaust images was neither adequate nor appropriate, and so we considered how to create a broader program within the facilities available to us. For some time, our parents had been planning

Making Memory

an extension of the property, and so we thought about utilizing some of those spaces and also developing new ones. The new building incorporated two levels, one subterranean, the other an open hall. We took early church and synagogue designs which often deployed polygons – usually octagonal – and created a sacred space for quiet and reflection. This was not an attempt to create a religious space per se, but a space that would engender contemplation and be reflective in nature. The plans to develop the project began to take place. We had determined early on that there was a need for non-Jews to make a more effective response to the Holocaust. Perhaps if we made this contribution, things would begin to fit into place and we could give the signal that this was of concern to everyone.

Wanting to do something to commemorate the destroyed Jews of Europe is one thing; having the competency to do so is another. We had little knowledge and no experience, so it was clear that we would have to do some learning fairly promptly. Without wasting time, we began to extend our own study, both formally and informally. We became engrossed in research and reading; we went on courses to Yad Vashem, further trips to Europe and the USA, and met with as many people who were running Holocaust centers as we could find. We also began to meet and talk with Holocaust survivors who shared their lives with us, and we sat down to discuss with educators and curators. Every conference anywhere that had the word *Holocaust* in its title, I was at it! The result was a steep learning curve, absorbing as much experience as possible, as quickly as we could.

We felt it was extremely important that whatever we chose to do, it should be seen as coming from outside the Jewish community. We knew that it was time for the world in general to make a serious effort to face a situation that it had helped create. As we thought about this, it became apparent that we might not have the right to do such a thing. The Holocaust is a matter very close to the Jewish community, and in particular to survivors and their families. What right had we to start creating memorial spaces and educational programs? What would happen if the Jewish community

~~Never Again!~~ Yet Again!

refused to accept the intentions of our effort and misunderstood what we had set out to achieve?

We struggled with this issue for some time, but reached the conclusion that the Centre should come from outside the Jewish community for a number of reasons. Firstly, the survivors had been badly let down for almost fifty years since the Holocaust was all but ignored by the Western world. Many had wanted to speak about their experiences, but had no one to talk to in the lonely years following their ordeal. Today we often reflect that survivors were silent. In actual fact, they were silenced. We felt it was important, if only for their sake, that Beth Shalom should clearly state that there were people outside the Jewish community prepared to take this on as their issue, to listen to those experiences and to deal with them openly and honestly. We knew that in so doing, we could not remove the burden, but at least we wanted to make it a little easier to bear. Secondly, we felt that other non-Jews should see this as their issue too, and take some encouragement from our own commitment to this work. It was all too easy for non-Jews, particularly in Britain, to feel sympathetic to the issue without it posing any real challenge to their lives, convictions, or actions. The Holocaust did not take place on British soil and therefore is not as embedded on the landscape there as it is on continental Europe. That is clearly to our advantage, except where it becomes the reason for detachment. We wanted to make the experience of the Holocaust less distant; to somehow find links and connections that would make people begin to connect themselves more readily to its reality.

Commemoration is naturally incumbent on those upon whose family lives the personal tragedy of the Holocaust casts a shadow. But we realized that to leave the survivors, their families, and the Jewish community to fulfill this duty alone was to desert the cause of humanity. We began to see our role as fulfilling a duty of some kind. It seemed there was a duty to provide commemorative memorial spaces within the context of British society for Britons to participate in, should they so desire. The Holocaust was not about the suffering of the Jews alone, but about the

Making Memory

suffering of humanity, as experienced by the Jews of Europe. To avoid the role of remembrance was to fail at a very basic level in respect of our duty as fellow members of the human race. The fact that Jews were murdered on Christian soil was even worse, and therefore the imperative to fulfill that duty was even greater. We felt a duty to commemorate the Jews of Europe, not as someone else's suffering, but as part of that in which we share as human beings. That said, it was not an attempt to dejudaize the Jews, to sanitize them of their Jewish identity in the cause of humanity. On the contrary, Jews died because they were Jews. That was the reason they needed to be commemorated.

I am often reminded of the Passover Haggadah, where each year Jewish families recite the ancient story of the escape from Egypt. What amazes me when I hear those words is that any Jew sitting around the table is reminded of his or her identity when told in no uncertain terms to remember that it was "I" and not "they" who came out of Egypt. In so saying, Jews commit themselves to their Jewish identity, as they reflect upon what their ancestors endured. Of course, they do not actually relive those precise circumstances, but the collective memory of the escape from Egypt is a memory that brings people together in communal identity. In a similar way, to remember the Holocaust is not only to remember that something happened in history, but also to identify with those who went through it. I am not suggesting for a moment a kind of vicarious memory of suffering and personal identification with the Holocaust directly. But by coming alongside and reflecting with those for whom the memory is very real, we can include ourselves in their community of memory, rather than observing as spectators from the outside.

The duty is not about the documentation of history – as important as that is – but about the way in which we remember the suffering of those who became the victims. The duty is not limited by creed, or color, or personal experience, but by the sense of injustice and the cause of humanity, which simultaneously recognizes that those potential victims suffered because they were Jews and suffered as human beings like anyone else.

~~Never Again!~~ Yet Again!

Not to remember them is to commit them to oblivion, to present Hitler and his accomplices with their final victory. If we do not wish Hitler to have that victory, then the commitment to remember is a key component for the future.

In addition to the duty of memory, there is also the responsibility of education. When I first confronted the Holocaust, I was stricken, but I did not feel personally guilty. How could I? I was not there. However, I did – and do – feel a tremendous sense of responsibility. The events are in the past and cannot be reversed. Society should nevertheless know about and be challenged by them. The responsibility is principally toward those who might not know, or make the personal effort to confront the reality of how serious this was – and is. Disseminating what we know as widely as possible is crucial to developing awareness and spreading knowledge. The responsibility is also principally focused on telling a generation too young to remember, too distant to make the association, too sheltered to appreciate its significance. It is the responsibility to ensure that one by one, we incorporate a wider group of people who understand the gravity of the Holocaust's consequences and formulate their own response to it.

The Holocaust did not take place in another time and another place. It took place in the here and now of human interaction, within the world of real people. It was therefore not an extraordinary event, but an ordinary event with extraordinarily tragic and disturbing consequences. For understandable reasons, we may have come to describe the Holocaust as an event virtually outside of human history, stimulated by our own desire to explain the extraordinary nature of what happened. Even the terms we use to describe it create a new language. The word *Holocaust* for a start, the Hebrew variant *Shoah*, Planet Auschwitz, *l'univers concentrationnaire*, the Tremendum, these are all terms used to describe an event that ruptures history by placing it outside the norms of linguistic usage. There is, of course, very good reason for this. How do you describe a gas chamber full of two thousand mangled bodies, which until a few hours previously had been

Making Memory

mothers and fathers, brothers and sisters, doctors, lawyers, rabbis, writers, poets, footballers, actors, musicians, and scientists? How do you convey, in "ordinary" terms, pits full of burning corpses? What about the children, the wise old people who should have graced our society today, who were thrown alive into the flames? Where do you find the words?

Our responsibility is not to lose sight of the fact that this happened. We see its outcome as extraordinary, and yet it was the result of making many small, ordinary steps. Through a gradual, step-by-step process, the Holocaust was carried out by individuals within the normal frame of human existence. Birkenau, Treblinka, Belzec, Sobibor, Chelmno, and Majdanek are not on another planet. When we read the harrowing stories of what happened inside the fences of Birkenau, or the barracks of Auschwitz, or the *Kommandos* (work details) of Majdanek, the whole world does not turn into a black and white movie. Inside the fences, red was red, and the sun was still in the sky. Outside the fences, the world kept on spinning and people lived their lives, notwithstanding the pressures of war. When the Nazis left "work" they smoked their cigarettes, drank their brandy, and talked of their day at the "office." They knew what they were doing, and they did it from day to day. Of course they had created quite unprecedented circumstances, but it was all carried out with deliberation. The conditions that seem so beyond our imagination were created and controlled by people who chose to do so. Our responsibility extends to ensuring that such choices are not made by ordinary people, with such extraordinarily tragic results, ever again.

Recognizing the duty of remembrance and the responsibility of education was just the first step; fulfilling it was another operation altogether. The initial problem was how to create a suitable memorial space in the middle of a field, in the middle of North Nottinghamshire. We were attempting to commemorate the destruction of the Jews of Europe two generations previously, a thousand miles away, with no sizeable Jewish community in sight. How could one connect it to the landscape and the society

~~Never Again!~~ Yet Again!

in which it occurred? A monument would not be the most appropriate or fitting means of fulfilling that duty. Monuments are more meaningful when linked to historical sites or publicly designated spaces. They often say more about the collective memory than they do about the events themselves. We did not want to create a passive piece of artistic representation which would be symbolic to the generation that went through the war, but would eventually lose its significance for future generations. It was more important to contribute to the education of a future generation than to create something emotionally or culturally satisfying for the present one. We spent time thinking about how to create the kind of space in which we could bring together people of all backgrounds and persuasions to confront the meaning of the Holocaust for history and for their own future.

We decided to create a "memorial environment" in which our principal activity would be education. We felt that we should not enforce any single perspective on the Holocaust, but rather present some basic facts, and act as facilitators to bring together people from across the spectrum of British society to confront the evil of the Holocaust and its consequences. Beth Shalom was to be a "house of peace" where we would provide a place of peaceful memorial in remembrance of the victims, and where we could also work together toward peaceful coexistence within our world through our education programs. It was our attempt to find a meaningful way of contributing to the discourse on the universal values of human existence.

Although the Centre we were creating was emanating from what was originally an institution with Christian links, we also felt it was important to avoid imposing a Christian reading of the Holocaust. So we made it nondenominational. To impose a Christian interpretation of the Holocaust would restrict its significance, its audience, and effectiveness. We did not want to limit its message, predicate its outcomes, overly complicating theological and philosophical agendas. Clearly, the Holocaust has profound implications for Christianity as a religion and for Christians as people. The Holocaust cannot be read in the context of Christianity, but rather Christianity needs to be read in the context of the Holocaust.

Secondly, we felt that the relationship between the visitors and the institution should be reciprocal and personal. We hoped that the visitors would teach us and shape the project through their reactions, feelings, learning, and research. We felt it would be limiting to create a prescribed learning experience, where visitors were told that "the lesson of the Holocaust is..." Even now, I do not profess to clearly understand what the lessons of the Holocaust are, and the moment I think I do, I believe I will have lost the ability to learn, and therefore to be effective. What we envisaged was a place that could confront the attitudes of the uninformed, but also be of value to those who knew more than we did. If the Centre was to be a genuine response to the Holocaust, it would be a place where that response would be shaped and honed by many new and difficult challenges, and by people from all walks of life who would benefit from what was there, but would also benefit the institution.

Thirdly, we felt that the Centre should be interdisciplinary since dealing with the Holocaust is interdisciplinary. If you are interested in theological responses to the Holocaust, how can you know this without first studying the history as history? How can you find out without research facilities? How will you understand the abandonment the Jews felt without reading the literature, filming the survivors, or investigating the philosophical reactions from a spectrum of thought before and after the outbreak of war? How can you understand the interpretations of theologians without reading the literature and documents that have emerged in the fifty years since? In other words, even to begin any topic related to this period of history, you have to enter an interdisciplinary world of learning and inquiry, and we knew we had to provide the basics for anyone wishing to start that journey.

Having decided what we wanted to achieve, James and I wanted to know what had been done in other places, and to develop our own learning skills. Our first port of call was back in

~~Never Again!~~ Yet Again!

Israel where we spent time at Yad Vashem. We both took part in the three-week intensive Graduate Institute program there. James followed the summer course and, due to constraints on my time, I followed later and did the winter course. While in Israel, we spent much time in the archives, the pedagogical resource center, and the library at Yad Vashem. We traveled to Beit Lohamei Haghetaot (the Ghetto Fighters' Kibbutz), near Nahariya, where there is a very fine museum and memorial. It was a particularly enriching experience to learn with young people like ourselves, as well as with more mature adults seeking to extend their own learning, and, of course, to do so with people from all walks of life and cultural backgrounds. At Yad Vashem, the delicate balance of national memorial, museum, education center and research institute is helpful in itself. Obviously, the development of those organizations demonstrated the need to fulfill the various roles through the creation of an institution that would be meaningful to Israeli society, to Jews around the world, and to the vast range of non-Jewish visitors who flock there every year.

Immediately after my few weeks in Israel, I drove through Europe with Penelle and Nicky, two Australian graduates from the seminar. We stopped at many sites, former camps and memorials: Bergen-Belsen, Berlin, Poznan, Chelmno, Warsaw, Lodz, Treblinka, Lublin, Majdanek, Belzec, Krakow, Auschwitz, Birkenau, Gross Rosen, Terezin, Prague, and Dachau. In each case, I spent time evaluating the ways in which the history had been written and confronted. There were many surprises, too. Up to this point, I was unaware of the lengths to which governments had gone, particularly in the Eastern Bloc, to twist the memory of the destruction of the Jews of Europe. Time after time, memorials failed to mention who the victims were, or prominence was given to general memorials to the "victims of the Hitlerite terror," as they often said. There are even specifically Christian memorials which all but deny the suffering of the Jews. I found this form of denial through the limitation of memory insulting and at the same time intriguing. Clearly, the effort to bury the past was purposeful. Then there was the eerie absence

Making Memory

of memory in so many places. It was as if there had never been Jewish communities in some places where once they had thrived. Then in small winding lanes we would find the tell-tale signs of doorposts where *mezuzot* had once hung, or faded Yiddish writing faintly visible through subsequent layers of whitewash. Yes, whitewash. In many ways that's how I began to see so much of this, as a whitewashing of the past. Obviously, there were those who hoped that a new, fresh layer would cover over that part of the past which was best forgotten. As I stood in those forgotten places, I felt that we should clearly state that even though they are forgotten, we have not forgotten that they are.

I then spent several weeks in the United States. The United States Holocaust Memorial Museum was yet to open, but I zigzagged from Los Angeles to Houston, to Detroit, to Florida and New York, and paid visits to no fewer than twelve institutions, all of which taught, documented, presented, and archived the events of the Holocaust. There I found an enthusiasm and a sense of purpose, both at local and national levels, that I had not seen elsewhere. To list those institutions and their achievements is worthy of a book in its own right. What amazed me was how much more had obviously been achieved in the United States than in Europe, despite its physical distance from the events. What was troubling was the tendency towards Americanization of the Holocaust. Interpretation of events seemed to be tailored to meet the demands of an American audience, who were sometimes only interested in what the Holocaust should mean to them as Americans, without a real understanding of its particularly complex European dimension. What I discovered was that in the vast majority of cases, these memorial institutions were either being created or funded by the Jewish community. This is natural, but it made them commemorative in nature, even when they supported important educational programs. It strengthened my resolve to ensure that the Holocaust Centre, Beth Shalom, should be different in that regard: while commemoration would be at the heart of the project, awakening a non-Jewish public from its apathy should always be the main objective.

~~Never Again!~~ Yet Again!

At a different level, seeing so many institutions run and funded by the Jewish communities of the United States, I did have some niggling concerns about our identity as non-Jews dealing with the Holocaust. I was also continuing to find the personal discovery of the Jewish tradition very interesting and attractive to me. The more I learned about the Jewish faith, the more closely I identified with it. Historical learning over a number of years was now coming together with a personal encounter with the Jewish community on a daily basis. James and I found we were developing many, many new friends within the Jewish community in Britain and further afield. There were often times when we would find ourselves in synagogue or at commemorations or celebrations. Our smattering of Hebrew was always helpful when trying to get the prayer book the right way up and eventually follow the services more adeptly. What was initially an interest in the Jewish tradition developed into a persistent question: "Is this becoming not only an interest, but also a way of life? Surely, if we are so closely allied to the Jewish community, its past and its future, we would be better off as a part of that community and its future. Should we become a part of this destiny and convert to Judaism?"

Actually, this interest had not developed from confronting the Holocaust, but from the previous years of encounter and learning, of which the Holocaust had become a significant part, bringing us even closer. James and I spent much time discussing this, in particular the theological implications of taking such a step. Is to convert to Judaism to desert the values of Christianity and deny the validity of the Christian message? If we do not feel theologically that we can convert, does it mean we are still allied to a supersessionist view of Judaism that will not allow us to "go backwards," and hence remains part of the problem? If one abandons the supersessionism and respects Judaism for what it is, what is there to prevent one converting?

There were added complications in this issue in that my parents' training in theology and a life's work of commitment to the Christian Church did not make it easy to broach the topic of conversion. We did spend a great deal of time talking about the Jewish tradition and the Holocaust, but actually to convert is a whole different thing. I was aware that my parents knew their theological principles fairly thoroughly; while there was little doubt about their encouragement of our goals, changing identity in the midst of all of this might be a step too far. Then my mother trumped me.

James and I were due to fly off to Berlin for a conference, and we had decided to meet from a variety of directions at Terminal One, London Heathrow Airport. My parents brought James to the airport, I flew in from the US, and we met up as planned in the lounge. As we sat there having coffee, suddenly, out of the blue, our mother piped up and stated, "Your father and I have been talking, and although we think we would be too old to do such a thing, we imagine with all you have been learning that you might one day consider converting to Judaism. We certainly wouldn't influence you on such a matter, as long as you know that should you ever choose to do so, we would not stand in your way." This came as an amazing surprise to me. Of course our parents knew about all our activities and interests, but we had clearly never dared talk about such matters as the theological implications of converting. While we lived in a home where faith was a key component of our lives, theology rarely was, at least not in terms of direct theological debate. However, I knew that for my mother to make that statement, having come from a conservative evangelical background, in addition to her own theological training, she had already weighed its consequences.

In the end we did not convert, but it was not for theological reasons. In fact, I would suggest that if any professing Christian is not comfortable theologically with the option of conversion to Judaism, then the question must be "Why not?" It should not mean that all, or any, Christians should feel the compulsion to convert to Judaism, but that there should be no theological reasons why not. Put another way, if a Christian disdains the thought of conversion to Judaism, then clearly such an individual still holds the anti-Judaic seed of antisemitism responsible for the context in which Nazism was able to grow.

~~Never Again!~~ Yet Again!

We did not convert because firstly, we became so wrapped up in what we were doing, we simply could not have found the time at that point. Secondly, we began to feel that part of the compulsion to convert was linked to our concern about the Holocaust, and we questioned the wisdom of that as a basis for conversion. I once commented that it would be more acceptable to be dealing with the Holocaust if we were Jewish. Jim's reaction was as clear as it was definite: "If we were to convert, we would lose the potency of our message and conviction, and therefore have much less to say." To be from a Christian background and prepared to confront the problem for what it is – that is something one has to be prepared to do, simply because it needs to be done.

We also felt it was important that the funding for the Centre's initial development should come from non-Jewish sources. We did not make any large appeal, but went to the individuals and groups who had previously been sponsoring the Centre and asked them to extend their generosity to the new project. We had also learned, over many years, that project work could make good use of volunteer professional and general labor, saving substantial costs. By disposing of one or two assets belonging to the charitable trust, we were able to help fund some of the capital costs. I was running a small business making miniature greetings cakes for birthdays and anniversaries. The profit from the business went into the project, too. This way, we were able to develop an important new project with relatively low costs and without having to approach members of the Jewish community with requests for initial funding. There was still a lot to do, but we were slowly finding the means to do it. The question was, could we really turn it into a viable reality?

Chapter Nine
Vision to Reality

There is a world of difference between planning something and making it actual, as we were about to discover. The Holocaust project was a vision, and we were inspired to aim towards what we wanted to achieve. However, it is one thing saying that you want to create a memorial and exhibition, but where do you actually begin in practice? It is one thing saying you wish to take this to the British public, but what happens if they do not wish to hear?

There was a particular concern with our audience. We were creating a project in the middle of the Nottinghamshire countryside, at a time when public perception of the Holocaust was still very low. *Schindler's List* was yet to happen, as was the fiftieth anniversary of the liberation of the camps, both of which were to have a huge impact a couple of years later. We sat down with all of our plans and aspirations and asked ourselves what would happen if we did all of this – and then nobody came or was interested. It was a telling question, not least because we had no reason to suspect that the British public would trek into Sherwood Forest to confront a history they perhaps considered was now well in the past, and therefore of little significance to them. We decided that whether or not people chose to come, it was still important that we undertook the project, if only to say that there is something you can visit and learn from, rather than nothing at all. If no one did visit, so be it; at least we would have tried. We were right and wrong to draw those conclusions. Right, because if we hadn't taken the risk, the Holocaust Centre would not be

~~Never Again!~~ Yet Again!

contributing all that it does today. On the other hand, we were wrong to say that it was all right to have an institution just to say it was there and provide the opportunity. For any place to have meaning, it must be relevant to a constituency that subscribes to its aims. In other words, it needs people to be a living institution. For that, one needs visitors who appreciate it. The visitors are its life, and without the visitors it has today, the Holocaust Centre would be of no value, as it would make no contribution.

We decided to go with a format that would allow a great degree of flexibility in terms of the spaces we had and their usage. We did not want the Centre to be a mere museum of the Holocaust: we didn't believe that any museum, however large, however well-resourced, however professional, could really do justice to either the scale of the Holocaust, or the personal tragedy that it represents. Therefore, we felt that the exhibition space should be limited to a relatively small area of the total, so that discussion spaces, lecture rooms, libraries, and learning facilities could provide our visitors with the opportunity to learn, to confront, and discuss the Holocaust and its meaning for their lives.

With this in mind, we also knew how important the exhibition would be in focusing and reminding the visitor just what we are talking about when we enter into discourse about the Holocaust. We wanted to create a thought-provoking and meaningful exhibit that would not just repeat known historical facts, but place them in a suitable context. We decided that our exhibit should be about people and how they were affected by history. It should not only be about *what* happened, but to *whom* it happened. We wanted to present the lives, the names and faces of some of the victims of the Holocaust. It seemed hugely important to create the right balance between presenting the numbers, which in themselves are highly significant, and ensuring that individual suffering was not misrepresented. How could one convey, in the confines of a small exhibit, what the history meant to one individual, not to mention to countless hundreds of thousands of families all across the European continent? I had come to realize that the Holocaust was not about the mass murder of six million Jews, but about the

Vision to Reality

suffering, the anguish, the fear, the pain, the murder of one Jew, and then another, and another, and another.

How does one convey to the average person with little concept of Jewish tradition and history that Jews in Germany were not the same as those in Holland, Greece, Czechoslovakia, and Lithuania? The vast cultural, linguistic, and religious diversity that existed across the spectrum of European Jewish life means that one cannot speak in this case of "Jewish suffering" in the singular. Somehow we have come to use the term *Holocaust* as if it were some kind of single experience that took place. This oversimplifies a very complex set of tragic events which affected and involved millions of people in very diverse circumstances over a long period of time. Clearly, the Holocaust was made up of tens of millions of experiences. To use the categories of "victims," "perpetrators," and "bystanders" undermines the complex nature of the way in which we identify individuals and their roles, and hence, what we can learn from them. To create pigeonholes limits the complexity of the experience and therefore restricts the lessons we can draw from it. Many victims were clearly only and always victims. But how far does the category of victimization stretch? Was a non-Jew lying on a bunk beside a Jew at Birkenau any less a victim of those particular circumstances? When he died in the night, was his death any less painful or significant than that of the Jew who died next to him? And what of the Jew who betrayed his fellow Jews? Was he a victim, a perpetrator, or a different type of victim? And what of the perpetrators? Some were only and always perpetrators. But what of the Nazi who helped Jews to survive? Is he less of a perpetrator, less of a Nazi, or the type of perpetrator that many were – complex human beings? Does that make his perpetration of crimes against other victims less or more terrible? And what of the bystanders? Could there be such a thing? Surely if you stood on the sidelines and watched, you too were implicated through your passivity, allied to the actions of the perpetrators through inaction. What was worse: a sworn Nazi, who genuinely did not know that Jews were being taken to their deaths, and did nothing? Or a cleric,

~~Never Again!~~ Yet Again!

dressed in the regalia of Christendom, who did know, and did nothing? And so one could go on, and on. It was not so simple, and to make it appear so is to underestimate the serious issues that lie within it. Somehow, we wanted to portray all of this in a meaningful way that would neither neglect the tragedy of the individual in the process of mass death, nor limit complex human history to simplistic analysis. We had to find a way.

We decided to create a "memorial exhibition" within the Centre that would not document everything we wanted to, due to space restrictions, but would commemorate at the same time as explaining. It would be an educational tool to focus the visitor on what the Centre is there to discuss, and why. In the exhibit, we would begin by introducing Jewish life in Europe prior to the Nazi period and try to show the young and the old, the rich and poor, the religious and secular, and give an insight into what their lives were like. We felt this was important as part of the context of the story we wanted to tell; after all, it was their story. One of the main frustrations we encountered was wanting to dedicate significantly more space than we had available and to present more about the history, traditions, and life of the communities that were destroyed. The question of who was destroyed seemed more significant to us than how it happened, though clearly it is important to know how it all occurred. We also wanted to avoid creating an impression of the Jews only as victims, particularly for non-Jewish people who may be unfamiliar with Jewish customs and tradition. True, all too often Jews have been the victims of Western civilization's penchant for antisemitism. But we felt that the life and soul, the struggle and dedication, the richness and poverty, that is, the diversity of the Jewish people, should be what captivated the imagination of an uninitiated audience, not their ultimate victimization. The problem of the victimization of the Jews lay with the perpetrators, not with the victims.

Nor did we want to create a perpetrator-focused exhibition. It is easy to utilize the documents, photographs, and footage of the Nazi propaganda units. It is comparatively easy to show how the

Vision to Reality

framework of destruction grew and developed through Nazi eyes. It is easy to show the mass graves and the piles of corpses. But all of these, real as they are, were what the Nazis intended to create. This was their world, their version of history. To recreate it seemed voyeuristic and totally unnecessary, however compelling the material. The Nazis were not interested in the communities upon whom they inflicted their venom; they had already reduced them to a "bacillus" in the body of the *Volk* that needed removing. As far as the perpetrators were concerned, the Jews were no longer human, so their version of history, their documents, photos, footage, and their memoirs are hardly going to illustrate their humanity. They are not interested in the feelings, the hardship, the resistance, and struggle for survival that Jews had to face every day of their lives. Of course, it is important to try to understand why the perpetrators did what they did. It is just as important to understand why so many chose the more convenient route of allowing the discrimination, degradation, and destruction of the Jews to occur right under their noses in their own backyards. We must also recognize that while a handful of people were able to muster the courage to care, there were clearly not enough of them to stop the tide of hatred. Finding out why some did have such courage might give clues as to why others lacked this amazing human quality.

In the confines of the exhibition, we tried to highlight the complexity of the experiences. As well as outlining the context of Jewish experience, we also needed to explain the context of antisemitism and its long, drawn-out history in the Western world, its absorption into political, social, and cultural structures, along with its development in Nazi ideology under the influence of the race sciences. This potent combination of antecedents is such that until the mass murder of Jews following the invasion of the Soviet Union in June 1941, very little was unprecedented in Christian history in the centuries prior to the Holocaust. Forced separation, social and religious isolation, the wearing of distinctive yellow badges, forced ghettoization, the burning of books and synagogues, restrictions on learning, professional practice,

~~Never Again!~~ Yet Again!

and intermarriage: these had all been visited upon the Jews before. This time, it was more ferocious, more precise, more final. We also wanted the exhibition to give voice to the eyewitnesses. The creation of opportunities to read the words or hear the voices of those who were there, and to enter into their experiences, became increasingly central to our goals. Through those experiences, we wanted to encourage our visitors to think about the real circumstances of real people caught up in the maelstrom of Nazi persecution. We wove into the text of the museum Holocaust survivor narratives and diary extracts in which the experiences of individuals, including survivors who volunteer to speak at the Centre, would be seen and heard within the context of the unfolding narrative of the Nazi era.

These include the reflections of Jewish diarist Chaim Kaplan, written at the moment of Germany's invasion of Poland. His almost prophetic words indicate just how much was known about the intentions of the Nazis:

> During the morning hours of the first of September, 1939, war broke out between Germany and Poland... For the time being Poland alone will suffer all the hardships of war, because there are no common frontiers between Poland and her allies. We are witnessing the dawn of a new era in the history of the world.
>
> As for the Jews, their danger is seven times greater. Wherever Hitler's foot treads there is no hope for the Jewish people. Hitler, may his name be blotted out, threatened in one of his speeches that if war comes, the Jews of Europe will be exterminated...
>
> The hour is fateful. If a new world arises, the sacrifices and the troubles and hardships will be worthwhile. Let us hope that Nazism will be destroyed completely, that it will fall and never rise again.

As Eastern Europe's new masters established ghettos for the Jews, the observations of the mayor of Czernowitz provide an example of non-Jewish reaction to what they saw. Their perspective

VISION TO REALITY

also seems important, if only to indicate just how much people really did know...

> I looked out of the window of my bedroom and amidst flying flakes of early snow, I saw a scene which was incredible. In the streets a vast crowd of wandering people. The aged were helped by children, there were women with infants in their arms, cripples dragging their lame frames. All had bundles, their hands were pushing small carriages, loaded with boxes. Some carried their burdens on their backs: luggage, bundles of linen, cushions, blankets, clothing, rags. They were beginning their mute pilgrimage to their vale of tears, the ghetto. The majority of the working-class Jews just wandered through the streets and alleys, pulling their pitiful barrows, carrying their miserable bundles and boxes until they sank exhausted in some corner or curbside and could go no further.

And from within the blinding circumstances of mass death, somehow some individuals had the strength to try to tell us what they saw, their reflections speaking right out of the camps and even the crematoria. The *Sonderkommando* who worked in the crematoria were entirely aware of the significance of the history in which they were involved. The *Sonderkommando* at Birkenau wrote in Yiddish or in special code, and buried what they wrote in the vicinity of the crematoria. Only after the war did the museum authorities overseeing Birkenau discover these notes, and among them, the words of Simon Lewenthal, which we used in the memorial exhibition:

> The history of Auschwitz-Birkenau as a labor camp in general, and in particular as the camp of extermination of millions of men will not remain – I am sure of it – sufficiently well handed down to the world. Part will be transmitted by civilians. But I think that the world knows a little about it even now. Surely for that reason we wrote it down...

~~Never Again!~~ Yet Again!

Finally, we also included throughout the exhibit a number of poems and reflections. Some of these were written by survivors and victims; others were not. We wanted to stimulate visitors to think beyond purely documentary sources and to have time, among the barrage of images and text, to stand back and reflect for a moment or two. Primo Levi and Dan Pagis are among the quoted authors, but perhaps most touching of all are the words of Franta Bass, one of the children of the Terezin ghetto, who wrote poems and drew pictures while in the ghetto:

The Garden

A little garden,
Fragrant and full of roses.
The path is narrow
And a little boy walks along it.

A little boy, a sweet boy,
Like that growing blossom.
When the blossom comes out to bloom,
The little boy will be no more.

One part of the Centre's plan was the garden. The Holocaust Centre sits in some three acres of Nottinghamshire countryside, on the edge of Sherwood Forest. Some say it is isolated, others that it is peaceful and quiet. Either way, it is well removed from the clamor of urban existence. In this setting, we thought we would try to create a peaceful and meaningful environment around the Centre, and so we created a garden. The garden is a counterpoint to the intense, stark images of the exhibition. In the quietness there is respect for the past, but also hope for the future. There are landscaped water gardens, with patios and areas for quiet contemplation. There is a memorial rose garden where hundreds of visitors have dedicated roses to the memory of loved ones lost in the Holocaust, or made general dedications of commemoration. A sculpture by Holocaust survivor Naomi Blake

Vision to Reality

is personal and provocative. Entitled *Abandoned*, the silhouette victim of Nazi persecution stands erect and dignified, asking the question, "Wherefore hidest thou thy face from me?" in protest at the abandonment of the Jews by God, yet full of the poise of a proud identity. Doreen Kern's *Anne Frank* and Stan Bullard's *Hidden Childhood* are pieces discreetly tucked into corners surrounded by foliage and garden aromas. Then there is the children's memorial, where thousands of visitors have placed stones in memory of the children murdered during the Holocaust. What I like so much about this memorial is that it grows and changes each day, and each day prayers, thoughts, and wishes are added, some by Jews, some by Christians, Muslims, Hindus, agnostics, or atheists. Every stone is there because someone wanted to remember by placing their own stone on the pile.

As we planned the Centre, we knew that we should not attempt to direct what visitors should think, feel, or say. We wanted to provide the opportunity for visitors to draw their own conclusions, think their own thoughts, say their own prayers, and to enter into whatever discourse they felt was appropriate for them as individuals. The memorial garden is a good example of how survivors, teachers, students, clergy, or laypeople can be themselves without the imposition of competing voices and images. Instead, they can take a break from images and spend time reflecting in relation to all they confront at the Centre. It is a place of beauty, of memory, and of hope.

CHAPTER TEN
IN THE PUBLIC EYE

January 1995 was the fiftieth anniversary of the liberation of Auschwitz and Birkenau by the Red Army. Somehow this had come to be a significant event in the public's perception of the Holocaust. I decided I would go to Poland to experience what happened there during the commemoration. I was not quite sure how to get close to what was happening, and so I called the Polish press office, told them I would be writing on the topic of the anniversary and asked for a press pass. I was told there should be no problem, and so I set off to Poland. That particular visit is another story in its own right, but while I was in the lounge at Heathrow Airport, I received a call from the *Jewish Chronicle* in London. They had been told about the forthcoming Holocaust Centre project and wanted to cover it that week in the edition which covered the fiftieth anniversary of the liberation of Auschwitz.

On my return from the commemoration at Auschwitz and Birkenau, there, sure enough, was a picture of the new Centre on the front cover of the *Jewish Chronicle*, just below the story about the fiftieth anniversary commemorations. It seemed strange to be suddenly thrust into the spotlight on such an occasion, not least because we had consciously avoided media coverage of the project until this point. We had not wanted the project to be "hyped" in the press for the sake of a story, because the content

~~Never Again!~~ Yet Again!

and substance of the Centre was, and always is, more important to us than media exposure, although of course we do want people to know.

The project, which was only a few months away from completion, suddenly took on a much more public dimension. The Jewish community was obviously curious about these developments. I was soon summoned to the Nottingham Jewish Representative Council to explain myself. The members listened patiently as I explained how the project had come about and what we hoped to do. At the end of my presentation, I wasn't sure what they would have to say about the imposition of the Centre in the vicinity of their community. However, the chairman, David Lipman, went out of his way to welcome the Beth Shalom project and expressed immense pleasure on behalf of the Council that it would be in the environs of the Nottingham Jewish community.

To my surprise, I found the Jewish community across Britain equally warm in its welcome for the initiative. What came across, time and again, was a sense of satisfaction that the Holocaust Centre was confronting the Holocaust from a non-Jewish community perspective and was prepared to tackle the issues with clarity and honesty. Of course, I am sure that any Jewish person in his right mind, on hearing that an entirely non-Jewish foundation was starting a Holocaust project, would question the motives behind such an initiative. There was little or no reason to suspect that any Christians would wish to take up the cause of confronting the Holocaust, and to do so honestly and with integrity, without at least some payback. We were simply telling the story because it needed to be told, and told well, to as many people as possible.

The general public was also somewhat circumspect. On one level, people were prepared to accept, listen, and take an interest in the Holocaust. *Schindler's List* had been screened in theaters by this time; the Holocaust was appearing on the school curriculum in England and Wales, and there was a growing awareness, particularly after the fiftieth anniversary of the liberation of the camps, that this was a real issue that still had not been fully dealt with. However, if there was to be a public expression of this, it might have been expected to come from Jewish sources in London or Manchester, and not from a rural province. Local opinion was also divided in the area: some saw it as an imposition on an otherwise idyllic rural landscape that did not need that kind of dark history. Others welcomed it as a fine asset to the area that would focus minds on important issues. The regional press took it to be an important local project, with national and international significance. What was clear, however, was that people of conscience would waste little time in beginning to engage the issues it raised, and would start to confront the Holocaust in a variety of ways in their schools, universities, churches, and clubs.

For us, the dilemma was how to combine our professional lives with the project that was our real passion. James was a young medical doctor; I made my living manufacturing celebration cakes. We had both maintained our own professions as we felt it important at that point not to earn our living from the Holocaust. We volunteered our time; we used the financial resources we had. This made life complex: I had to leave my business unattended at times and James had to work long hours as a doctor, and then still contribute to the life and development of the project. At the same time, we wanted to ensure that we didn't underestimate the necessity of being totally professional in our work on the Holocaust. We decided that we would work as a family team to run the Centre. Our mother worked in the team with us and managed the day-to-day working, coordinating the administration, our survivor volunteer team, and visits. James continued his career for a while, but after a year or two, planned to take a couple of years out of his medical career to work full-time at the Centre. Ten years later, he is still on a "short break" from his medical career! I was to teach there virtually full-time, but leave some provision for maintaining my business. Somehow, we have achieved a great deal with this combination of roles. Because we were prepared to work for each other, as well as with each other, I think our diverse lives have been rewarded, if at times they become a little pressurized.

~~Never Again!~~ Yet Again!

Prior to opening the Centre itself, we launched a traveling exhibit entitled *Another Time, Another Place*. This was initially made available to schools. Very soon, we found that the exhibition was booked up months in advance, with some 250 young people each week benefiting from it. This interaction with schools before the Centre's opening created the foundation of important relationships with schools across the country, which would generate almost instant demand when we began our operation.

Finally, on September 17, 1995, the day came when we could say that Beth Shalom, our house of peace, was ready to challenge the British public with the need to remember the Holocaust and to assume its responsibility to teach and warn future generations. In our minds, there was only one person who could possibly open it: our friend and mentor, Professor Geoffrey Wigoder, who was a fine scholar and had embodied so much of the Jewish-Christian dialogue since the Holocaust. He had supported and encouraged us throughout our planning and creation of the Centre, yet it would be his first visit to the site. Our guests that day came from all across the spectrum of British society, and among the audience were a great many survivors, for whom the Holocaust Centre became more than just an exhibition about a period of history in which they were involved. In many ways, it became their own place of memorial, their own Beth Shalom.

CHAPTER ELEVEN

FROM PAST TO FUTURE

There is a huge difference between the world that existed during the Nazi occupation of Europe and the one that young people inhabit today. It doesn't carry the same danger, the same uncertainty, or the same weight of concern. Young men are not at war while their womenfolk work in the fields and factories; we do not need to carry ration cards or dig bunkers in our gardens; ghettos, gas chambers, and transports to "the East" do not impose themselves upon this particular generation of Europeans. Most children live in a world that is safer, more sheltered, and more protected, although sadly this is not the case for all. Naturally, we crave that safety for them; we work for it, protect it, and uphold it. But with safety comes complacency. Cocooned in the relatively secure environment of the early twenty-first century, how do we convey or envisage something as removed from most people's personal experience as the Holocaust? It is one thing talking about the ghetto and explaining its mechanisms – the starvation, the disease, the fear of death, the overcrowding, the will to live, and the courage to resist. These can all be described, but how do you really understand their implications? How does a teenager living in the comfort of North America or Europe relate to the utter deprivation and dehumanization of life in the concentration camps?

As the distance of time from the events unfolds, how does one bridge the gap between what happened in the past and how we

~~Never Again!~~ Yet Again!

imagine it today? How do we teach a younger generation, detached from that past, and make it make sense not only within their world today, but within their future too? What can we do to ensure that our message does not trivialize the Holocaust, or turn it into a series of clichés that unintentionally belittle its complexity? These were the kinds of questions we were asking before the launch of the Centre, knowing that many of our visitors would come with little or no prior understanding of the historical detail of the Holocaust.

One key question we had to answer was what kind of format we wanted to adopt in representing the Holocaust to our respective audiences. We decided initially not to be a public gallery, allowing the public to visit the World of Robin Hood in the morning and "do the Holocaust" in the afternoon. We wanted visits to be structured, educational, and interactive. Our visits have largely been structured educational seminars. Whatever the background of the group, whether it is from a school, a university, or a church, the Centre encourages visitors to engage with the topic, at their own level, rather than passively looking on. Each visit is structured to open up new ways of exploring, researching, thinking about, or discussing the Holocaust and its meaning for their own lives, careers, or perspectives. Six years later, the decision was made to open to the public, too, in order to allow greater access to that broad group of people inadvertently excluded by our policy to focus on an in-depth quality experience.

The Centre is now open as a museum to the public, but the main focus remains with education and training groups because we can give a deeper encounter, allowing more time and greater focus. We achieve this by working as closely as we can with the group leader to ascertain the background and interest of the group. If they are a group of thirteen-year-old history pupils, their needs are likely to be different from those of a group of senior year high-school students studying moral philosophy, or a graduate museum studies group, a Jewish student group, or a group of senior clergy. The diversity of backgrounds necessitates

Top: Holocaust survivor Joanna Millan talks to primary schoolchildren in the memorial rose garden at the Centre

Left: Steve Green, Chief Constable, Nottinghamshire Police, 2000 – 2008; under his leadership, Notts Police incorporated seminars at the Centre into their training program

Bottom left: Majdanek survivor Pinchas Gutter returns to the camp for the first time with his children; their journey was captured in the Holocaust Centre's documentary *The Void*

Kindertransportee Dorothy Fleming addresses teachers in the memorial hall

Above: Survivor Kitty Hart-Moxon signs copies of the revised edition of her testimony, Return to Auschwitz

Left: Survivors Ibi and Waldemar Ginsburg with a graduate from Lithuania at the Beth Shalom-Yad Vashem Summer School

Left: A school pupil working in the memorial exhibition

Below: James, a medical doctor by training, is also accomplished in multimedia, here working on the creation of a CD-ROM in the Centre's design studio

Left: Swedish Ambassador Mats Bergquist, accompanied by myself and survivor Gina Schwarzmann, opens the Gateway of the Righteous on the occasion of the Centre's Sixth anniversary

Below: Receiving an MBE for services to Holocaust education, 2000

Bottom: Discussing the exhibition with HRH the Duke of Kent on his visit to the Centre, July 2001

Above: Survivor Arek Hersh with members of a Beth Shalom party outside a church in Sieradz, Poland, where in 1942 he was parted from his family forever. He was told to join a work group, but his family was deported to Chelmno.

Above: Victoria Vincent tells her story to several young actors. Sadly, she passed away three days later. Their memory of her story then became her legacy.

Left: Rabbi Emeritus Lord Immanuel Jakobovits at the children's memorial, accompanied by his grandchildren

Below: The children's memorial, where visitors can place a stone in remembrance of the 1,500,000 children whose lives were so needlessly wasted

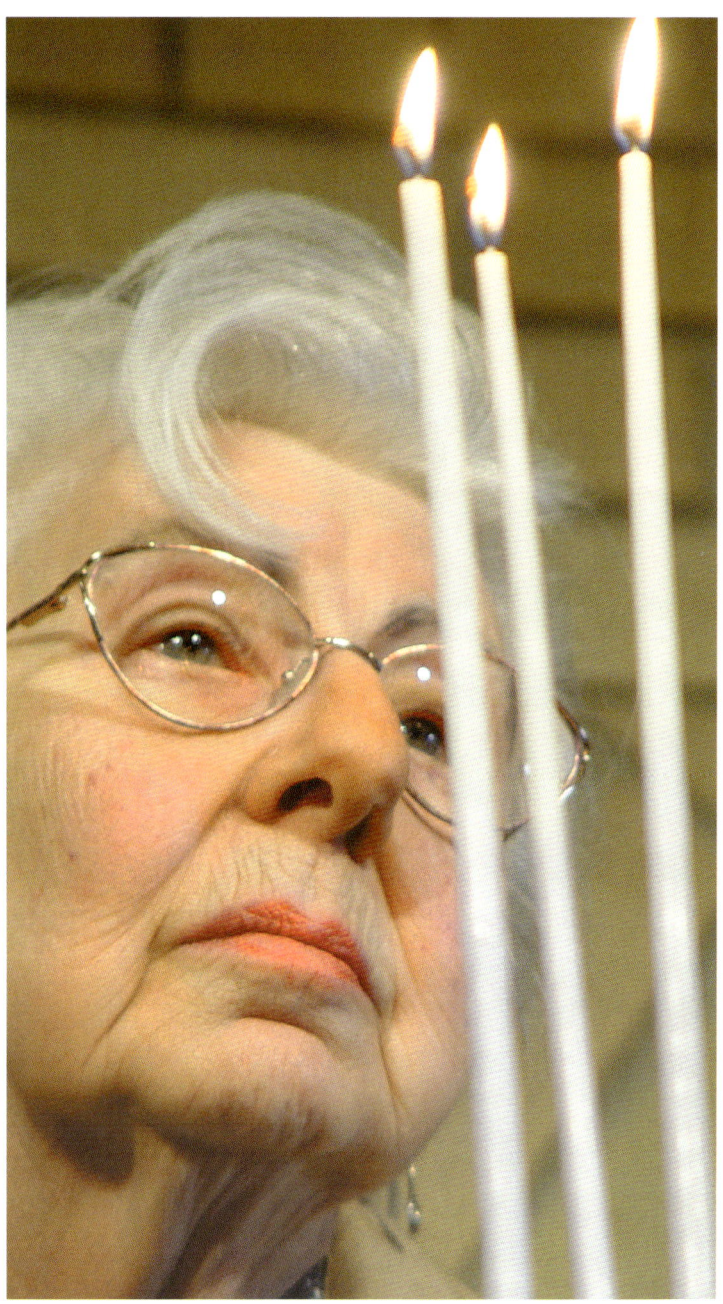
Auschwitz survivor Trude Levi, lighting a candle at Beth Shalom's Yom HaShoah ceremony, 2002

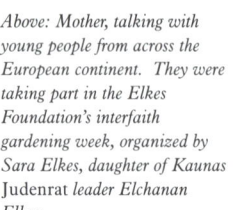

Top Right: Bergen-Belsen survivor Rudi Oppenheimer lighting a candle at Beth Shalom's Yom HaShoah ceremony, 2002

Top Left: Sam Pivnik, a survivor of Bendzin, Poland, stands by the images of 653 people from his hometown, most of whom perished

Below: Friends and colleagues from Lithuania, most of them non-Jewish scholars dealing with the Holocaust in education and the media

Above: Mother, talking with young people from across the European continent. They were taking part in the Elkes Foundation's interfaith gardening week, organized by Sara Elkes, daughter of Kaunas Judenrat *leader Elchanan Elkes.*

Above: Addressing a group of visitors in the hall

Right: School pupils arriving at the Centre

Below: Hidden Childhood, *a memorial donated by Simon Winston in memory of the Jews of Radzivillov who were brutally murdered by the Nazis in 1941–3. Sculpted by Stanley Bullard, 2001–2.*

Top: Architect and artist Roman Halter, a survivor of Auschwitz, in his workshop. Roman worked with his son Ardyn to create the Holocaust Centre's four round stained-glass windows, three of which are shown above.

Right: Sir Bob Geldof, a patron of the Aegis Trust, faces the TV cameras during a visit to the Holocaust Centre, 2002

Below: Artifacts from the Holocaust Centre's collection. The spoon of an unknown victim from Kanada, Auschwitz-Birkenau; and the suitcase of Lotte Kramer, a child who survived the Nazi onslaught thanks to the Kindertransport.

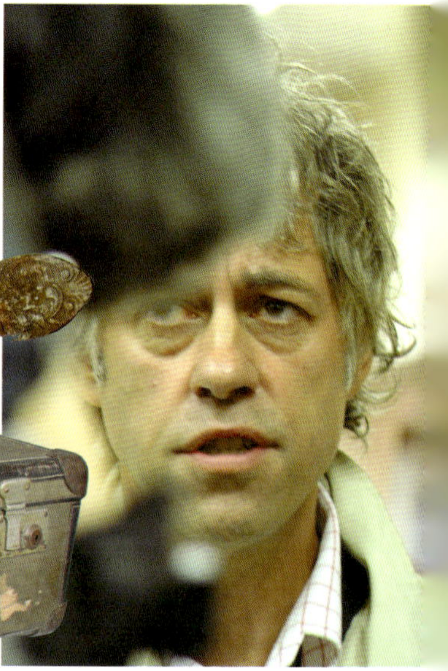

From Past to Future

a different starting point, a different set of focuses in discussion, and different sets of goals and outcomes for the visit.

I will outline the visit of two different types of group to show how varied the needs and interests can be. The Holocaust is taught to eighth-graders in UK schools, in the history curriculum. History classes will tend to come to the Centre in relatively large groups and need to fulfill their curriculum requirement to learn about the Holocaust. The students themselves tend to be very diverse, with a wide range of abilities and cultural backgrounds. The vast majority will know very little about the Holocaust. Prior to the visit, we will work with the members of staff concerned to prepare the pupils as well as possible within the time constraints, encouraging teachers who have not visited the Centre before to do so ahead of the school visit in order to better prepare the students. It is important that the students know where they are going and why, and what is expected of them.

The visit, which will last between three and five hours, is divided into three parts: historical exploration, understanding the personal tragedy, and analysis and discussion. On arrival at the Holocaust Centre, such a group will initially see a twenty-minute introductory film about their visit and its aims. This is illustrated with archival images and covers the main historical points. It also demonstrates historical sources and encourages students to make full and appropriate use of them while investigating the Holocaust as history. They are also encouraged to think about the questions that the history of the Holocaust raises for them. The students then divide into smaller groups, one group in the exhibition, the other working with audio-visual presentations. If there are three groups, the third will work in the memorial gardens or other temporary exhibitions. The groups rotate until each has completed all of the activities. At this age, students will usually work in the exhibition with an analysis-type worksheet to encourage them to consider carefully what they are seeing, and to begin the process of thinking it through. After a break, they will then spend an hour listening to a survivor relate his or her personal experiences, and try to get a sense of how this broad

~~Never Again!~~ Yet Again!

history affected one person, one family, one community. This is a significant part of their visit, for at this point they enter into the real lives of real people. Following that session, a survivor and one of the Centre's professional staff members will, wherever possible, lead discussion with the group and try to develop a discourse around the issues that emerge from the experience. Very often, questions are directed at the survivor, certainly on issues such as forgiveness, faith, and beliefs (which incidentally are the most common question areas for pupils of this age). The visit does not seek to draw conclusions from the Holocaust experience, but tries to raise the type of questions students are likely to need to continue to ask, for their immediate study and much further beyond.

Alternatively, if the Centre is addressing a group of twelve ordinands who will shortly become parish priests and are attempting to come to grips with the Holocaust as part of their training, they have a very different set of criteria to fulfill. As with the school group, we will, of course, consult with the group leader, or tutor. On arrival, such a group will have a more question-based introduction, conducted by a senior member of the team. The questions we pose focus around the causes of the Holocaust, including the long history of Christian antisemitism, the historical context in which it took place, and the kinds of issues it leaves in the contemporary world – in particular, in relation to the Christian environment. We may also talk about the origins of the Centre, using that to focus on the underlying issues that stimulated it to come about and why. Through the challenges I encountered as a theology student, for example, I am able to convey some of the challenges they may want to consider. It is also important that a group of this kind understands the global issues the Holocaust presents, particularly for those in positions of moral and social influence. After an introduction, the group will spend over an hour in the exhibition. They will also usually hear a survivor speak, although for a shorter time, as discussion forms an important part of their encounter. After discussion with the survivor, we will spend time in workshops reflecting on what has been encountered during the visit and how that might impact upon their own learning and future professional life. In particular, we will investigate the meaning of the Holocaust for Christian thought and practice, including the persistence of Christian anti-Judaism, the Jewish-Christian relationship and the challenge it might pose to their future congregants.

The diversity of the two groups illustrates the need to be able to address the same historical scenario from a variety of perspectives. Other groups that attend the Centre might cover as wide a spectrum as youth workers, race equality officers, police officers, military personnel, victim support groups, rotary clubs, etc. Our training department now leads these visits and has a particular emphasis on working with professionals who impact directly on the community, to highlight the issues pertinent to their values and their work. Clearly, in the personalized and more intimate surroundings of a small, focused Centre, individual needs can be more readily met than in a museum designed for hundreds of thousands of visitors. The goal of the Centre is not only about raising awareness – although we hope we do just that – but also about challenging those who are already aware regarding just how much – or how little – they have really questioned and explored the meaning of the Holocaust for their own lives and professions.

PART THREE
REFLECTIONS

PART THREE – REFLECTIONS

CHAPTER TWELVE

LEGACIES

For fifty years we ignored them. Maybe we didn't know what to say. Maybe we didn't know how to say it. Perhaps we were just too busy building our own lives to care what had happened to others "during the war." Just after the end of World War II, when victory was being paraded in the streets and relief swept over the long-embattled leaders of the world, among the debris of the conquered Third Reich were the remnants of the otherwise obliterated Jewish communities of Europe. The disease-ridden, starving band of survivors, who by a roulette combination of luck and design had avoided otherwise inevitable death, had now emerged from the abandoned death camps. Their suffering, long ignored by the Western world, suddenly became the focus of postwar propaganda efforts. Week after week the words "Now we know what we were fighting for..." broadcast to Saturday matinee cinemagoers, explained with perfect aplomb just how little they had really known what they were fighting for at the time. They certainly had not been fighting to liberate the camps or to save the Jews, but of course no one was going to admit that once victory was secured. And the survivors sat in displaced persons camps, without families and without friends, without a past or a future. But now, at last, they were certain that the world would want to hear.

The Allies demonstrated their resolve to deal with this past by instigating war crimes trials for accused members of the Nazi hierarchy. Some were hanged, but the vast majority received

~~Never Again!~~ Yet Again!

relatively light sentences for their crimes. Once the trials were over, the public suitably informed and the process of judgment at Nuremberg concluded, the world could then refocus its attention on rebuilding the future and forgetting the past, not to mention facing the threat of its new Communist enemy in the East. And still the survivors sat in the DP camps, waiting for someone – anyone – to give them a home. Those who did not go to Australia, Canada, the US, or Britain began finding their way to Palestine, where, of course, once the State of Israel was founded, they thought everything would be all right. Actually, we now know that the Israelis were not very much better at listening to the survivors who arrived from the camps. They had a nation to build, and they needed strong resolve to face the future of survival, not their past. And so the survivors had much to say, but no one to whom they could say it.

Today we have grown used to survivors in our midst. We film them, we tape them, we publish their memoirs, and make films in their names. Day in and day out our media cover stories of long-lost relatives, restitution, and the fight for a dignified end to what was an undignified beginning. Yet somehow we still struggle to understand exactly what they went through, and what it should mean to us.

In the years running up to the opening of the Holocaust Centre, I had come to know a number of survivors around the UK, and had started to forge important working relationships with several individuals in particular. Kitty Hart-Moxon, Ben Helfgott, Trude Levi, Paul Oppenheimer, Abraham and Vera Schaufeld, Gina Schwarzmann, and Victoria Vincent are among those who gave enormous encouragement to our efforts prior to opening, and there are too many to name subsequently. Our intention to document and include parts of their experience in the exhibition in turn led to discussions about the importance and place of survivor testimony in teaching about the Holocaust. I was aware that it remains a special privilege to be able to share with survivors: though they are in their latter years, they remain willing and able to tell their all-important stories to a generation

Legacies

for whom otherwise there is little with which to grasp such reality. Naturally, survivors cannot and do not tell the whole history of the Holocaust. Survivors tell their own particular experience as they have come to remember it. But from that comes an important dialogue across generations which can move, warn, and highlight the consequences of prejudice and the road to mass death.

Survivors themselves are aware that nobody's memory is perfect and that every detail will not necessarily be retained or accurate. Survivor testimony is not a replacement for learning the history of the Holocaust, but it is a personal perspective which the historical facts alone cannot convey. The Holocaust is not only comprehended through its overwhelming enormity, but also through the enormity of its consequences for individuals. It is not only told through documents, but through voices, confusion, anguish, and deep sorrow. At the Holocaust Centre, it is important to us that as many young visitors as possible – and most adult and professional groups too – have the opportunity to hear a survivor speak, not only to hear what happened, but also to talk about the consequences and meaning of the survivor's story for their own lives in the contemporary world.

Among all the stories of survivors who became involved with the Centre, that of Victoria Vincent is particularly moving. Victoria called me one day to see if she could come to the opening of the Centre, and in the course of the conversation, I asked if there was a particular reason why she wanted to come. She explained that she was a survivor of Birkenau and Auschwitz, and now lived in Nottingham. I went to see her soon after and found a lady in a wheelchair with a medical history that read like a medical student's textbook. We sat together as she told me her story. I realized from the way she shook as she talked that she had rarely told the story before. It was only later that I discovered I was virtually the first, after her husband and doctor, to hear her tell her experiences. I suggested she should write her story down sometime and, to my surprise, she told me that she had already done so, for the benefit of her grandchildren. Several weeks later,

~~Never Again!~~ Yet Again!

we published her story, *Beyond Imagination*, as a memoir and educational text, and it became an important part of our library of resources. Over the next year, Victoria, who was otherwise virtually restricted to her home, traveled the country visiting schools and universities and spent many, many hours at the Centre. When she died a year later, I found that I had lost a very dear and personal friend. I also discovered that the privilege of sharing with survivors today is one we must not underestimate. The conversations we shared, and those that I have subsequently shared with many of my survivor friends and colleagues, remain some of the most important learning experiences of my life.

Soon their lessons will be legacies and we, the generations that follow, will have to carry the message they are trying to convey. That message is not just the experiences they endured, but what those experiences have come to mean. Out of the initial interaction between survivors and students, survivors and professionals, survivors and the media, survivors and the process of documentation, I soon began to realize that beyond testimony there is another layer of the relationship as yet not fully explored. In placing survivors in front of video cameras and asking them to say what happened to them, we create another document. Of course, that document will be invaluable to future generations and is therefore very significant. Those in the future who need to know what happened will be able to access wonderful, technologically sophisticated archives such as we have at the Shoah Foundation Institute for that purpose.

However, survivors have another story to tell: that is the story of how they have come to understand their own experience – and we need to know that story, too. Whenever a survivor tells his or her own story, he or she selects a number of episodes that have particular meaning. It might be about the loss of a loved one, or the day they realized that their fate was sealed. It might be about resistance or defiance, or justifying a certain act that may seem morally dubious in the "normal world" outside the circumstances of the Holocaust. It might be about God, or human nature, or evil or good. Whatever the case, behind the text of the story are many perspectives that may not at first be apparent. In dialogue and discussion, these perspectives emerge and can develop into important and revealing conversation.

In bringing young people together with survivors, it is important that a conversation take place beyond the telling of the story itself. In this way, I hope that survivors of a generation who suffered the consequences of state-sponsored genocide can share with the decision makers of the next what they understand by the experience and what may be learned from it. This is a fundamental principle, not least because the legacy that survivors leave is more than the narration of what happened to them: it helps us to make sense of all they endured and suffered.

The urgency to do this is clear. The passage of time will eventually take its toll and we will be left guessing about answers to questions we never thought to ask. Voicing those questions now and entering into discussion with survivors who are willing and able to contribute their reflections is, I believe, an important role for centers such as the Holocaust Centre, Beth Shalom, to fulfill, along with all the other establishments and colleagues who care about these issues. They are witnesses, and one day we will have to convey their legacy. Through these dialogues, I think I share the hope of many survivors that in sixty years' time, young men will not have to stand in front of audiences as old men, weeping as they tell stories of the complete destruction of their families, friends, and communities.

CHAPTER THIRTEEN
LANDSCAPES OF MEMORY

The Holocaust has not always been the prominent part of the cultural landscape it is today. In fact, its development as an issue has been somewhat slow in coming. The Holocaust Centre, Beth Shalom, entered that slow development late in the day, although remarkably it was the first such venture in Britain, and perhaps the first in the world to emerge from its particular perspective.

Initially, Yad Vashem, created in the early 1950s, emerged as the memorial that provided a necessary and important focus for survivors and Jewish communities the world over. Then the Eichmann trial in Jerusalem in 1961 started the development of public discourse in the light of the Holocaust. This happened first in Israel, and was followed by a slow but steady stream of responses from a variety of places and disciplines. Survivors had tried to speak, but it was scholars in the late 1950s and early 1960s who were researching the period of the Holocaust. Through their study and publications, they began creating the makings of a recognizable historical discourse on the Holocaust. Raul Hilberg, Israel Gutman, Karl Schleunes, Lucy Dawidowicz, and Yehuda Bauer, to name but a few, produced seminal texts still read and reread today. Then, in 1978, Gerald Green's docudrama *Holocaust* was screened on American television and in other countries around the world. The film was roundly condemned by the survivor community as a fiction and a poor

~~Never Again!~~ Yet Again!

attempt to portray anything like the real situation – with very good reason, as it was a fictional story and a serialized drama. However, from that point onward, Holocaust studies, representations, museums, and education programs began to grow with increasing rapidity. In the last thirty years, we have seen a virtual explosion of writing, creating, building, and dialogue around this difficult topic.

It did not happen all at once, of course; there were milestones along the way. In 1978, President Jimmy Carter instituted the United States Holocaust Memorial Council which, fifteen years later, resulted in the United States Holocaust Memorial Museum. That same year, in November, Kitty Hart-Moxon took a British film crew to Birkenau and for perhaps the first time, a survivor described in some detail to an audience all around the world what had happened to her and hundreds of thousands of others like her. In 1985, Claude Lanzmann, who had been filming in Poland for some ten years, released his nine-hour, testimony-based film, *Shoah*.

From that point on, there was little to stop the growth of interest. The fortieth anniversary of the liberation of the camps in 1985 was given time on television and radio, and public conscience began to grow. Films, books, memoirs, literature, analysis, history, theology, philosophy, oral history, and audio-visual testimonies all started to emerge in greater and greater quantities. Conferences that previously had struggled to attract informed and interested audiences were occupying larger and larger hotels and halls. When, in 1988, Elisabeth Maxwell organized an international conference entitled "Remembering for the Future," hundreds of scholars from around the globe converged on Oxford, and the field of Holocaust studies took another step toward general acceptance in the academic world.

Then the museums began to open. In America, the city of Detroit was the first to open a center with an exhibition and education facility in 1978. Thirty years later, there are over 250 members of the Association of Holocaust Organizations, most of them American, many with museum exhibits. Education institutes and bodies also began to develop rapidly. Organizations such as Facing History and Ourselves, the Anti-Defamation League, and the USC Shoah Foundation Institute, and recent State legislatures in the USA, have taken it upon themselves to ensure that students in particular are given opportunities to confront the Holocaust while they are young. Associated with this are important programs in teacher training and graduate-level studies, and, relatively recently, the first master's program in Holocaust Education at Richard Stockton College, New Jersey.

In Europe, of course, the situation was more complex because postwar the continent was divided. The Soviet Bloc sat like a huge immovable monolith on the doorstep of a confident but still confused West. Scattered across the topography of the European continent were hundreds and thousands of camps and sites of mass destruction, where the myriad victim groups of the Second World War had been murdered or worked to death. Holocaust memorialization and education emerged as European governments decided what to do about these dark stains on their landscapes, and how to explain to young people how they came to be there. On the whole, they preserved them, paid for their upkeep, and installed curators and museum designers to ensure that information was available for the curious public. However, the messages, particularly to the young, were very mixed. West German children learned history, history, history. Polish children learned that Auschwitz was the site of the martyrdom of Poland under the Nazis. The Soviets learned about the greatness of the Red Army in its heroic struggle to overthrow fascists who were murdering Soviet citizens. And the British learned virtually nothing.

Then in 1998 in Sweden, a survey was conducted by Helene Loew into the attitudes of young people towards far-right ideology and movements. She discovered that over twenty percent of Swedish young people had some concern about the veracity of the Holocaust, or knew that it was questioned. Almost five percent said they thought there may be some doubt about it. This gave a serious jolt to the then Swedish prime minister, Göran Persson. He instigated a project called *Levande Historia*

~~Never Again!~~ Yet Again!

(Living History) to teach about the Holocaust, its causes, and consequences. Living History published a book written by Paul Levine and Stephane Bruchfeld, entitled *Tell Ye Your Children*. It was offered to the families of high-school students free of charge. Overnight, it became the second most owned book in Sweden.

Persson was determined to introduce Holocaust education into Swedish life and he contacted President Bill Clinton and Prime Minister Tony Blair to invite them to support his initiative. I was contacted out of the blue by the Foreign and Commonwealth Office (the UK equivalent of the State Department) one Friday afternoon, to see if I was able to travel with them to Sweden the following Monday for a meeting. Somewhat taken aback, I agreed, not really knowing why I would be going to Stockholm with the Foreign Office staff, when previously I had never spoken to a government official at any level about anything to do with the Holocaust. I was there with Professor David Cesarani and Lord Greville Janner, representing the UK. It turned out that Professor Yehuda Bauer had seen the delegation list from the UK and wondered why I was not on it, hence the late invitation. At the meeting, there was also a small delegation from the USA, including colleagues from the United States Holocaust Memorial Museum.

We waited as Göran Persson stood up to address us in the small lecture theatre. I was skeptical. What could a politician possibly add to the work we were all engaged in? I thought he would not have anything useful to say. I could not have been more wrong. Persson spoke with personal conviction, political clarity, and practical application. He wanted us to think more deeply about how government could help to make the message of the Holocaust clearer, and in particular to focus on education. When it was my turn to speak, I abandoned my notes and responded to Persson's points directly. We were now engaged as scholars, educators, survivors, and politicians in a single mission. Persson invited the delegations in attendance to form a small group as an International Task Force for Holocaust Education, Remembrance, and Research. First the USA and Britain joined, followed very quickly by Israel and Germany. Yehuda Bauer steered this task force into being, supporting Persson as he went, ensuring high standards of academic rigor and pragmatism.

Then the plan was developed to invite a group of countries to an intergovernmental forum to discuss Holocaust education, remembrance, and research in Stockholm. I was one of the three academic advisors to the Stockholm Forum 2000, along with David Cesarani and Yehuda Bauer. When the letters went out to over fifty countries, inviting their heads of state to attend, I do not think anyone on the team expected the response we received. Twenty-two heads of state accepted the invitation. Of those countries that did not send heads of state, ironically it was the first two countries in the task force – USA and Britain – who sent the lowest-ranking politicians – an undersecretary of state and the foreign minister.

The planning for the Stockholm Forum 2000 was meticulous. Working behind the scenes, I saw the whole mechanism at play. I was privileged to work with Yehuda Bauer and the team in the Swedish Prime Minister's Office, preparing the detail and working on the format for workshops that would bring diplomats, politicians, scholars, and nongovernmental activists together to discuss Holocaust remembrance issues.

On January 27, 2000, there were approximately 1,000 delegates in the hall, listening intently as speeches were delivered by the delegations. There had been some discussion as to whether to let this stream of speeches occur. But it was decided that it was important for each delegation to put on record its policy about Holocaust education, remembrance, and research. Not many people made it from dawn to dusk listening to the fifty-five countries deliver their position statements. Predictably, there was repetition about the importance of the Holocaust to human civilization, about not repeating the same mistakes in the future, about being prepared to teach the next generation. Mainly superficial commitments and hackneyed clichés. However, what was important was the fact that each country was going on record, stating its commitment. They were also addressing their own

~~Never Again!~~ Yet Again!

electorate. Whether or not the newspapers of Lithuania, Belarus, Hungary, Bosnia-Herzegovina, and a host of other countries reported the speeches, I am not sure, but the speeches were intended for them.

Tony Blair did not attend the Stockholm Forum. However, he used the day to make an announcement in London. Attending the opening of the Anne Frank exhibit in London, he announced that Britain would launch a national Holocaust Memorial Day in 2001. Foreign Secretary Robin Cook simultaneously announced the UK government's commitment while addressing the Stockholm Forum. This was a significant step for a country that had been part of the conspiracy of silence. Britain was committing itself to remembrance.

As I collapsed on my bed that evening in the hotel in Stockholm, it was clear that fifty-five years after the Holocaust, the world was changing its attitude. Until that morning, the complaint had justifiably been that the world had forgotten its duty to remember the Holocaust. Whatever happened in that room, that was no longer the case. Now there was a new question. "Now that the world has committed to remembering the Holocaust, what kind of memory should it be?"

Back in Britain, plans started to be drawn up for our first Holocaust Memorial Day commemoration on January 27, 2001. A steering group was drawn up by the Home Office – the Home Affairs Department – which included a number of individuals and organizations involved in Holocaust education, and in related areas such as gay rights, disability, equality, and ethnic minority groups. The steering committee met every month and grappled with the question of what kind of memory should be presented to the British public.

The format we developed for Holocaust Memorial Day fell into three sections. There was to be a national ceremony, a community program, and an education program. The national ceremony was to be centrally organized and senior figures would be invited. The rest of the activity was intended to be driven by grassroots activists. At the time, we had no idea how successful this format would be. We also spent time discussing the scope of this day.

There are only three problems with *Holocaust Memorial Day* as the title for the day. They are *Holocaust, memorial* and *day*. *Holocaust,* because it implies that it is exclusively about the Holocaust, although actually we made a very clear decision that the Holocaust would be firmly at the center of the commemorations. However, we also made clear from the outset that Holocaust Memorial Day would address issues of contemporary relevance, as well as the range of genocides that have taken place since the Holocaust, including Cambodia, Bosnia, and Rwanda among others. This is clear in the guideline for the day, but not in the title itself. The problem with the word *memorial* is that it implies something retrospective and static. But the activities are proactive, educational, and community based. Commemorations do take place, but we encourage people to participate in their communities, to use their voice, to become empowered effectors of change. And the word *day* is a problem too, because the work we do goes on throughout the year. We run conferences and produce class resources that have all-year-round relevance, and we want the message of Holocaust Memorial Day to be one that people live with every day, not just on one day.

Despite those drawbacks, the impact of Holocaust Memorial Day on British society has been quite exceptional. In 2009, there were more than 550 registered events and over half a million people that we know of participated. That does not include school-based assemblies and commemorations – and over 3,000 schools requested commemoration packs, which were free of charge but only distributed on request. As chair of trustees of the Holocaust Memorial Day Trust from 2005 to 2010, I had the privilege of watching as year after year, British society continued to surprise us with its interest and dedication to Holocaust education and remembrance.

Today, all across the world, there is an ever-widening community of people attempting to find ways of breaking down barriers between people and their memories, and building

~~Never Again!~~ Yet Again!

educational programs that will bring people together to share in a common tragic past. Skeptics would argue that the process is driven by politics, commercialism, and the containment of memory. In part they would be right, and great care is clearly needed to avoid such pitfalls. However, there are now serious centers and programs dedicated to teaching about the Holocaust across America, throughout Europe, and as far afield as Australia, Argentina, and Japan. Wherever there are people who really care about the values of humanity, people who share concern over our failures in the past and our direction for the future, there you will find someone who cares about the Holocaust and its impact on our conscience.

Following the demise of the Soviet Union, new opportunities exist in former Eastern Bloc countries, where archives have been opened and those responsible for tending sites of mass destruction are reevaluating their message, not least because travel has become so much easier. Aside from the institutional changes that are taking place, younger academics are beginning to address the topic of the Holocaust as their own concern, and its teaching is more widespread. Naturally, one has to be patient. It takes a long time for any nation to come to terms with its past, and for many of these countries the legacy of Communism is still a more pressing issue than the legacy of the Holocaust or the persistence of antisemitism.

However, through my own experiences I have come to encounter many courageous individuals working in the field of Holocaust studies who are presently making enormous strides. By way of example: in Lithuania, a country still struggling to assert its own post-Soviet identity and all too keen to minimize Lithuanian collaboration with the Nazis, it is easy to suggest that there is little hope for a serious program of education and remembrance about the Holocaust. On the contrary. As in most situations, there are two sides to the story. While Lithuania has many internal and external controversies, and the collective memory is predisposed toward antisemitic stereotypes and accusations, a growing group of historians, educators, sociologists, and journalists are slowly

LANDSCAPES OF MEMORY

forcing a confrontation within society that will eventually impact upon what can be spoken of, where and how. Perhaps as a result of these strides and the serious engagement of the government there, Lithuania is able to take a leading role in working with other countries in the region, to help document, commemorate, and teach that difficult part of this past. My own experiences in Lithuania of teaching teachers and working with interfaith groups and academics have been enriching and stimulating, with Lithuanians now incorporating their Jewish heritage more readily.

In South Africa, the Cape Town Holocaust Centre opened in August 1999. While the UK Holocaust Centre was a non-Jewish initiative, the Centre in Cape Town was developed by the visionary and very determined Myra Osrin. She arrived at the Holocaust Centre in Nottinghamshire after a three-continent tour to see Holocaust museums, in search of inspiration. She toured the Centre with me. Afterwards, I told her that creating the Centre had taken considerable time and effort, and that if there was anything she wanted that we could provide, it would be our pleasure to assist. Through her leadership, the city's small Jewish community has created a potent and powerful confrontation with the history and causes of the Holocaust for the benefit of general society. I was pleased to work with Myra, her able design team and the trustees of the new center. Together, we created a small permanent exhibit and education facility in the heart of Cape Town. It has made a huge contribution in a country where young people in particular need to build a more tolerant society in the generation after apartheid. In dynamic environments such as South Africa, it is important not to project external perspectives onto communities that have their own complex societal issues, but that those who are willing and able to confront their own past, make sense of history, and make their own bridges for the future should be given every support possible. The Cape Town Centre's success can be seen in the recent adoption of the Holocaust onto the national curriculum in South Africa, and the creation of the South Africa Holocaust Foundation – a group of

~~NEVER AGAIN!~~ YET AGAIN!

three linked institutions in Cape Town, Johannesburg, and Durban. Richard Freedman, director of the Cape Town Centre, and Tali Nates, director of the forthcoming Johannesburg Holocaust Centre, are running centers and education programs that will have deep and long-lasting consequences for a society previously torn apart by racism.

These examples demonstrate that learning about the Holocaust and its meaning is not only an issue for the countries where the events happened and historical perspectives are embedded in the landscape. Those of us who are geographically removed have exactly the same learning process to go through, so traveling to the sites of destruction, to places such as Germany, Poland, or Lithuania, is instructive, life-changing even. Not only does one see what happened, where, and to whom, but one also understands further what and who was destroyed, what few remnants are left, and one can learn from the discourse and dilemmas in those places today. I am not talking about "Holocaust tourism," those visits made purely out of voyeuristic curiosity, or so brief that they cannot possibly be meaningful. I mean rather, the kind of visit which allows time to confront and understand the world that once existed there, which probes thoroughly the consequences of Nazi occupation. It should try to understand the shape of the communities who lived there, why others in the vicinity did not do more, and why the population finds that history hard to face today. The visit should also give sufficient time to contemplate the awfulness of forgotten places like the many forgotten killing sites – Zbylitowska Gora, for instance, or the larger sites such as Chelmno, or Ponary. I also believe that visiting such places without meeting and talking with the people of those countries today is to place all of us in the path of danger once more. We have to learn to speak with one another at these places, to communicate and be honest about our fears and anguish; otherwise the hurt will never heal.

It is easy to say that Poles or Lithuanians or Latvians are antisemitic. If all we do is say it, walk around, then leave, we can write off the Polish-Jewish relationship. It is much more difficult to identify the lingering antisemitism, and then be prepared to work with those open to learning. A constructive dialogue can be engaged – and indeed it is – but we have to be willing to engage. If antisemitism is a problem in Poland, discourse, dialogue, and education should be encouraged all the more. Organizations such as the Association for Polish-Jewish Relations in London, where Jonathan Webber, Ben Helfgott, and others have worked tirelessly to improve relations, have shown remarkable strides. On the trips I frequently make to Poland, taking groups of students and teachers, we make a point of having a mixture of Jews and non-Jews to visit sites of former Jewish life and sites of mass destruction, and to meet those in Poland today who are actively engaged in the social discourse. This, I believe, is where our future lies.

CHAPTER FOURTEEN
THE JEWISH-CHRISTIAN RELATIONSHIP

Cain and Abel provide the archetypal story of jealousy, competition, and murder between brothers. The story goes that Cain slew Abel and then attempted to absolve himself of responsibility for the crime he had committed. "Am I my brother's keeper?" he responds to God's inquiry about the whereabouts of his younger brother. Cain's answer was not to answer. Since the conclusion of the Second World War, among the many unanswered and perhaps unanswerable questions, one in particular challenges a reassessment of the state of relations between the Church and the Jews: "Why does your brother's blood cry out to me from the ground?"

The problem facing Christians following the mass destruction of European Jewry is perhaps best understood as that of inadmissibility. Jews were murdered because they were Jews, and all of this in the context of a nominally Christian environment. Wholehearted opposition from the Christian Churches to the so-called "Jewish policies" did not happen, and so Christianity is in some way implicated, along with everyone else, in the crimes and their outcomes. However, merely to highlight the shortcomings of the Christian world might suggest that it had some moral high

~~Never Again!~~ Yet Again!

ground prior to the Holocaust. The crisis of credibility must only be a symptom of a more fundamental problem. Did Christianity lose credibility because of its failure to act, or was it fundamentally flawed in the first place? Further, and more troubling, was the Christian environment in some way causal, providing a basis or a context in part, on which the Nazis could build their anti-Jewish policies?

I began by explaining that an important factor in the creation of the Holocaust Centre was a recognition of the need to address the Jewish-Christian relationship in its contemporary context. Now that the Centre is fully functioning, and is used by Jews and Christians (and many others of course) on a daily basis, the question is how the Centre can contribute to that relationship.

The questions are disturbing if you are a practicing Christian. But they are questions that must be asked. The facts reveal that few Christians during the period itself demonstrated "christian" behavior, although conversely, many non-Christian people were entirely "christian" in what they were prepared to do. Ironically, the very religion that had lent its name to the virtues of moral humanitarianism was largely unable to demonstrate such qualities at a personal level; and it certainly did not do so as an institution. Since the Church did not take the lead in instructing its Christians how to behave, the christian Christians who did take action did not demonstrate the credibility of their Christianity, but rather their own humanity.

We understand the individual's demonstration of goodness by what she or he was prepared to do. It required saving someone, helping to hide someone, or risking one's life to oppose injustice in some way. It meant doing something that was not required of anyone, but still needed to be done. In times of crisis, statements are considered sufficient for an institution to demonstrate a particular position, and to indicate its position to its membership. For the institutional Church to be effective, it had only to speak and its duty would have been fulfilled, at least in part. The silence of the Christian world clearly indicates apathy at best, and connivance and collaboration at worst.

The Jewish-Christian Relationship

Some ecclesiastical institutions made vocal, public, and official stands against Nazi policy. The vast majority did not. The lack of understanding, leadership, or care in respect of the persecution of the Jews during this period amounts to purposeful negligence. Negligence occurs when a clearly defined and understood responsibility is overlooked, with reckless disregard for the consequences. The Christian Church cared neither about the Jews as people, nor about what happened to them. Church negligence implicates it as an accessory to the outcome of the persecutors' actions; silence was complicity and participation.

The failure to understand the relationship between Judaism and Christianity – except in terms of longstanding enmity – ensured that Christian clergy were not equipped to evaluate their moral and fraternal responsibility, and furthermore often justified the persecution of the Jews as divine retribution. The Jews were the "other" and that "otherness"' was sufficient to salve their conscience of any personal liability. If individuals can justify their (in)action through their ideology, clearly the theology behind it is questionable. How can people feel at liberty to behave in such a way and still feel able to call themselves Christians? The failure of professing Christians to act on behalf of the Jews demonstrates the abject failure of Christianity as a religion and Christian people as its representatives.

The bravery of the few "Righteous among the Nations" stands therefore as a real example of human behavior. The fact that many among them were practicing Christians, including priests, pastors, and bishops speaking out against the Nazis or assisting the Jews, illustrates the possibility of "christian" behavior during the period. But their relatively small numbers begs the question, "Why were these righteous people of Christian persuasion acting of their own volition?" Their presence demonstrates the possibility of "christian" goodness. That they were few in number may also demonstrate that it is only to be expected in relatively few cases.

The solutions to these desperately serious failures require Jews and Christians to do more than dialogue in a newfound friendship, desirable as that may be. Apologizing and moving on

~~Never Again!~~ Yet Again!

will not address the fundamental fault lines that have developed in the Christian tradition. Christians have difficult realities to face, which can no longer be ignored. In short, Christianity has to go back to its origins, its texts, its theology, and dogma and take a thorough review. If it is not able to do this, its relationship with Judaism – and by extension with Jewish people – will never be better than a distant truce.

For Jews, of course, the issues are entirely different. The presence or absence of God, and his ability to act or intervene, or his choice not to do so, are more likely to test the relationship between Jewish individuals and their faith. For some Jews, just to reassert the continuity of belief and accept suffering as nothing to do with the divine is the way to keep faith in spite of the Holocaust. For others, to protest to God or about God is the only way of keeping faith, while also letting their anguish or complaint be heard. Either way, Jews are faced with issues concerning the continuity of the tradition, the maintenance of identity, and the challenge of the future of the Jewish people.

In the Christian environment, the discourse has centered around antisemitism, with good reason. Christians do not struggle with the nature, omnipotence, omnipresence, or revelatory power of God in the context of their relationship with the Holocaust. Christians struggle with Christianity. They need to, but in so doing, they also avoid the real theological disruption of the Holocaust. In fact, one may go further and suggest that much of the Jewish-Christian relationship engaged by Christians is about the defense of Christianity, rather than facing the challenge it poses. The problem is, all Christians are Christian by conviction – Christianity is a choice. Jews are Jews, whether they like it or not. To profess Christianity is to justify it and defend it, because at the point when you challenge its relevance, you either cease to believe, or you believe something else.

Until Christians are prepared to face the possibility of losing Christianity in the light of the Holocaust, there can be no meaningful Jewish-Christian relationship. For this to exist, Christians must struggle with their own identity and memory, and be

The Jewish-Christian Relationship

confronted with the possibility of nothingness. This sounds harsh, but in the light of the mass murder of European Jewry, not to face that potential is an insult to the lives of the victims. I would say that there is no meaningful Jewish-Christian relationship because Christians have not yet put Christianity on the line as it should be. Dialogue does now exist, but dialogue is relatively easy. A relationship is something that is not formed in words (although words are important too), but in common understanding, shared experiences, and aspirations. Jews and Christians have not achieved that yet.

As a contribution to repairing this broken relationship after the Holocaust, the Holocaust Centre highlights serious issues for Christians. This is partly because the Centre sets an example to Christians that facing the implications of the Holocaust need not be feared. It also continues important work carried out throughout this century, in confronting the long history of antisemitism which is deeply embedded in the Christian tradition.

It is in the face of this that the Centre attempts to be a symbol of care, where care about the past has been all too absent; a gesture of good will after centuries of ill will; a sign of hope in a hopeless situation; a means of conversation when words have no meaning. The Holocaust Centre is not an admission of guilt, but a sign of responsibility. It is honest about the past and concerned about the future. And in that most troubled of relationships, Beth Shalom hopes more than anything to be a place of peace.

CHAPTER FIFTEEN

THE HOLOCAUST AND THE FUTURE OF WESTERN CIVILIZATION

The questions remain unanswered, "How should the Holocaust impact upon our lives in the contemporary world? Are we studying, investigating, uncovering this because of the past, or because of an underlying concern about the future?"

The destruction of European Jewry as a historical event within the context of Western civilization is reason enough to spend time, energy, and resources to better understand what happened and represent it to a wider community of people. Whether or not there are lessons to be applied from that history, it is important for any individual who is moved to contribute to a meaningful commemoration of the Jews of Europe. Their lives and talent were wasted, their contribution, or simply their presence within the communities of Europe, was a sufficient loss for us all to feel the effects and mourn them as our own.

Behind these events that trouble us so much are a number of causes we recognize. These unseen or often unaccounted-for causes are the real concern, because without them, men, women, and children would not have been gassed and burned. Clearly, without

~~Never Again!~~ Yet Again!

the ambitious leadership of Hitler, or the pernicious race ideology that singled the Jews out for destruction, none of this could have happened. But it took much, much more than that. There were literally thousands of agents who instigated, orchestrated, or carried out the murders. There were millions of individuals, active or passive, who helped the process along, or who did nothing. Of greatest concern in all of this is that despite claims that the Germans were predisposed to doing such things, the vast majority of Germans who were involved made the kind of choices that anybody might make in the same situation. Over a period of time, they were able to carry out barbarous crimes against humanity and feel no sense of shame or guilt; on the contrary, they saw themselves as contributors to the great Aryan good.

Anyone can create a dream civilization: the utopia to solve all the ills of the world. Then, provided there are sufficient beneficiaries from what that civilization has to offer, the losers, the persecuted, or the destroyed will not matter. The ethical considerations raised by this are very clear. Historically, the victim's experience of genocide is always different. What is disturbing is that the mechanisms of perpetration and the reaction of the bystanders in such crises are generally quite similar.

One of the questions we asked ourselves in setting up the Centre is how we could contribute to a better understanding of the path to genocide. It seemed important to alert our visitors to the fact that although they might feel that everything in their own lives was going smoothly, the path to genocide begins in unsuspected places, and every act of intolerance and discrimination must be taken with the utmost seriousness.

A fundamental question to ask in regard to personal responsibility and ethnic persecution is, "When does one start to intervene?" When the gas chambers are burning and the trains are arriving daily? When the ghettos are full and their inhabitants starving to death? When war begins and villages are torched and synagogues burned? When political leaders threaten mass murder? When, and if, war begins? When persecution drives people from their work and children from their schools? When

Responding to the Kosovo crisis, April 1999: planning the appeal (right), sorting the mountains of aid donated by the public (below), and delivering the aid to refugee camps on the Kosovo-Albania border (bottom right). With media, public, and business support, within eight days the East Midlands Kosovo Appeal was able to dispatch fifteen truckloads of aid.

Above: Retracing with Kitty Hart-Moxon the route of her death march across Poland for the BBC documentary Death March: A Survivor's Story

Below: Filmmaking is an increasing part of the Centre's work

A range of resources, literature, and films produced at the Centre

Myra Osrin: founding director of the Cape Town Holocaust Centre

The Cape Town Holocaust Centre: Beth Shalom set the tone for the creation of this new development, initiated by Myra Osrin, and remains an admiring partner

Black children in the townships, from communities that will be learning about the Holocaust through school visits to the Cape Town Centre

Anna-Karin Johansson and I discuss the Living History project, initiated by Swedish prime minister Göran Persson in 1997

Images from the inaugural National Holocaust Memorial Day. Inset: Survivor Anita Lasker-Wallfisch talks with liberators of Auschwitz and Bergen-Belsen, General Vasily Petrenko (left), and Major Dick Williams, during the HMD ceremony at Beth Shalom, January 2001.

Top: Lilian Umutoni, Kigali City Authority's manager for the project, discusses the future genocide memorial center in the empty buildings at Gisozi (left) with Jim; 250,000 victims of the genocide are buried in close proximity

Below: Clothes of genocide victims at the Murambi memorial center in Gikongoro province, southern Rwanda. At least 40,000 people were murdered on this site in April 1994.

Rwanda 2002: Surrounded by children while filming (top); genocide survivor at Bisesero (left); bones and clothing still lying in Ntarama Church where the victims were murdered in 1994

Top: Foreign Office Minister Peter Hain presents General Romeo Dallaire with the inaugural Aegis Award, January 2002

Right: Aegis Executive members Richard Rubenstein, Carol Rittner, and Hubert Locke with Linda Melvern, author of A People Betrayed: The Role of the West in Rwanda's Genocide

Bottom: Delegates take part in the landmark Aegis-FCO Genocide Prevention Conference, January 2002

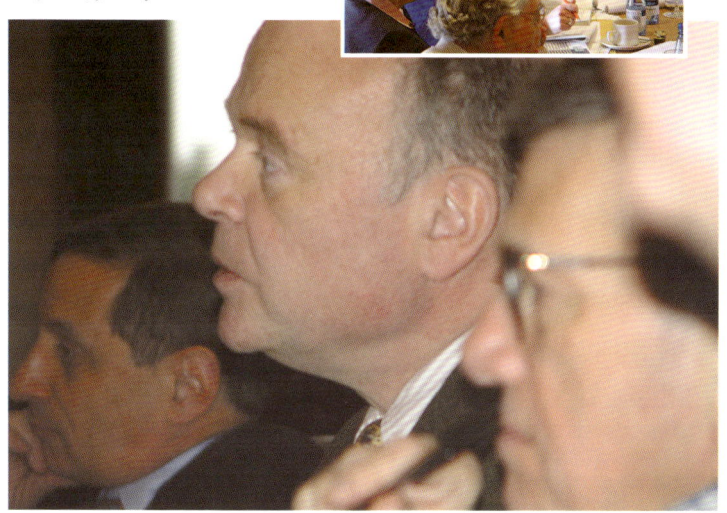

James listens to a presentation during the Aegis-FCO Genocide Prevention Conference, 2002

Lessons from Rwanda, *an exhibition created by Aegis in conjunction with the UN Department of Public Information, was launched in New York by the secretary-general in April 2007*

Rt Hon Clare Short MP, formerly the UK's International Development Secretary, and John Bercow MP, now Speaker of the House of Commons, speak in Westminster at the launch of the Protect Darfur campaign, March 2005. Photo: Geoff Pugh.

The Holocaust and the Future of Western Civilization

laws dictate who can and who cannot be citizens? When parties include the threat of ideological persecution in their election manifestos and make the scapegoats of a faltering society a matter of public concern? Or is it when somewhere, at some time, you hear a remark about "them," those people considered outsiders, who might just become the scapegoats in the manifesto, who may no longer be citizens of their own country and are driven from their jobs and schools, who are threatened with death, whose villages are torched and synagogues burned, who are starved in the ghetto and daily put onto trains and burned?

When we can answer this, I believe we will be better placed to say that we have understood the Holocaust. It does not undermine the immense tragedy we are trying to commemorate, nor detract from the singular importance of understanding the enormously complex issues that surround the Holocaust as a historical experience. It simply reinforces the understanding that at the time of the Holocaust there were simply too few individuals who understood enough, or did enough, early enough. So often we say that we did not know what was happening in Europe during the Nazi occupation. But in actual fact, the events of April 1933 should have been enough. The question is whether or not they would be, even today.

In our quest to understand, we knew we should be careful not to oversimplify things. When I try to comprehend the Holocaust, I know that I struggle to come to terms with it for a whole variety of reasons. Historically, I know that it is an event I will never really understand. A set of events that took place over twelve years, in over twenty countries, involving literally millions of people, I know is beyond me. I could spend my life trying to understand the complexities of Weimar Germany and its transition to the Third Reich, and the metamorphosis of the German people with it. I could spend my life studying occupied Poland, or France, or Greece. And having completed my research on a chosen topic, I might well draw my conclusions, only to admit that after a lifetime of research, a great deal was still left unclear.

~~Never Again!~~ Yet Again!

Similarly, I know that I will never really understand the personal tragedy of the Holocaust. I spend much time with survivors, listening to their heart-wrenching stories and trying to comprehend the pain of survival and all they have had to live with. When writing the foreword to the book of my good friend Waldemar Ginsburg, I found myself with a real dilemma. Here is a man who sat with thirteen members of his family in Kaunas, Lithuania, in June 1941, deciding whether to flee to the Soviets or stay under the occupation of the Nazis. Older members of the family had experienced German occupation in the First World War and could vouch that the Germans were civil enough then. Younger members of the family had just returned somewhat disillusioned from the Soviet Union. And so they decided to stay in Lithuania. A few years later, he was the only one of that family group still alive. So, as I sat down to write, I had to ask myself what right did I have to write the foreword to a book containing experiences I clearly cannot understand? What do I know of starvation and thirst, incarceration in the ghetto, working in the winter cold with little protection, mass shooting, selections, and the struggle for survival, day after interminable day? And what do I know of having twelve members of my family shot, beaten, dragged away in front of my eyes, or pushed overboard at sea? What right do I have to write about such things?

I found that I had no right to do that.

But I also found that I do have a responsibility, if only to try to explain how little I comprehend such things; how much I struggle to conceive, let alone relay, issues relating to the Holocaust.

There is something I do know. I do know that the Jews, as the victims of National Socialism's campaign of discrimination, isolation, deportation, and mass death, were not appealing to other Jews to come to their assistance at that time. In any given situation of persecution or mass death, the victims are never best placed to act as advocates on their own behalf. In a genocidal situation, agents are needed outside the victimized group who are prepared to act or intervene on their behalf. If the Jews of

The Holocaust and the Future of Western Civilization

Britain, America, and the Yishuv in Palestine could have done a little more, or been more alert, aware, and prepared to speak out, then that would have been for the better. Like everyone else, the Jews of the free world of the time need to examine their conduct closely. However, the Nazi Party was not likely to listen to a group of Jews in New York telling them how to run their antisemitic racial state. What was required was the conscience of the world, of governments, of academia, the media, and all those who cared about the fate of others to speak out and make an impact upon the situation. That does not mean that they would have been successful, or that the outcome would have been any different. But at least we could have said that we tried, that humanity had its day, and that no stone was left unturned in a bid to do whatever was possible.

Those voices of conscience were not there; the Jews were not a priority for the governments of the day. Blame for the total destruction cannot be leveled at anyone except those who carried it out. Responsibility for the unhindered manner in which that genocide took place lies squarely with those who were silent.

All of these rather sweeping conclusions are fairly easy for me to reach, as I am a generation removed from the events and have the benefit of hindsight. And I am not best placed to make such judgments. Firstly, I was not there and do not know how I would have reacted. I would like to think that I would have been the one who wrote the all-important letter that changed public opinion and rallied the masses to the aid of the Jews. I would like to think I might have been the politician in power who would make the vital speech and change government policy towards a more humanitarian outcome. In reality, I suspect that like the vast majority I would not have known what to do, or would simply have chosen to do nothing. Secondly, in my adult lifetime there have been a number of genocides or genocidal situations. One was in Bosnia-Herzegovina, others in Rwanda, Darfur, Congo, and East Timor. In terms of their historical significance, one might argue that they were not on the same scale, nor as long and drawn out, nor the long-term ramifications as serious as for

~~Never Again!~~ Yet Again!

the Jewish communities of Europe whose whole civilization was all but wiped out. Of course, they were not the same type of genocide as the Holocaust because no two genocidal situations are the same. What concerns me, however, is what I did about them. Because I didn't do anything of substance about either Bosnia or Rwanda. I wrote a few letters and made a few calls as people were dying – no, being murdered – in my backyard.

If "evil triumphs when good men [and women] do nothing," and if I consider myself "good" in any way, some kind of action is required of me when I see something evil happening. If this is a "lesson of the Holocaust," it is a demanding one: it requires you to act on behalf of somebody else. Then you look at those people who did do something and, in spite of their actions, evil is still seen to have triumphed. Was their goodness less good than the evil, or were there insufficient good people to outweigh the evilness of the evil people? Or did the few evil people have more who were willing to follow their example than the good had to follow theirs? If one thing we learn from the Holocaust is that we are required to act, another is that we might not be successful in our efforts. That does not mean we should not take action, otherwise the Righteous among the Nations were wasting their time and no one will ever do anything like that again. But be prepared for a thankless task, because if we succeed and genocide becomes a thing of the past, no one will ever know it did not happen. And if it continues, our detractors will only point out our failure to be effective.

I am struck by the human message that this contains. While the Holocaust itself might have been unprecedented in human history, the motivating forces of racial discrimination and ethnic hatred are a universal phenomenon in which the potential to repeat mass death may lie in wait for any number of future unsuspecting victims. The upside is that the will to resist that demonstrated itself so powerfully is also a universal principle that can be motivated for the common good. The question we must ask, as educators and facilitators of our history, is how to encourage the principles of ethical choices, political and personal

The Holocaust and the Future of Western Civilization

action on behalf of those vulnerable to mass killing within the societies in which we live.

It was the Easter holiday weekend in 1999. Hundreds of Kosovar Albanians were being massacred and tens of thousands forced out of their homes and country by Serb forces, against which NATO was waging an air war. James and I realized that as directors of an institution claiming to address the issues raised by the Holocaust, we could not ignore the situation. We initiated the East Midlands Kosovo Appeal, both as an expression of our concern, and as a means of concrete practical action. Perhaps a little to our surprise, this sparked such an overwhelming public reaction that within several weeks we had hundreds of volunteers working around the clock in a 15,000-square-foot warehouse filled to the ceiling with aid, with trucks leaving daily delivering hundreds of tons of aid for the refugees camped in Albania and Macedonia.

People from all over the region where we lived turned out, offered their homes for refugees, and offered their time, their trucks, their voice, their goodwill. It seems to me that our goal in Holocaust education is not to prevent genocide against Jews as a consequence of antisemitism, although that is obviously part of it. It is to prevent the waste of human life, anywhere, at any time.

There is suffering the world over. Each person's suffering is different because human suffering cannot, must not, be compared. This is not about who suffered more, or less, than anyone else because what one individual suffers, another feels equally in another time and place. The Holocaust Centre does not document the suffering of the Jews because Jews suffered more, but because Jews suffered. In this world of troubling and oft-repeated persecution, we do not need comparison, we need compassion.

Chapter Sixteen
What Next?

As a result of the East Midlands Kosovo Appeal, James and I traveled out to Kosovo, Albania, and to Macedonia in different capacities. James went out to be a volunteer physician for the International Medical Corps. Based in Kukes, Albania, he and his colleagues were involved in helping with the refugees who had flooded into the town, and in repatriating the Kosovar Albanians after the conflict came to an end. I found myself on several occasions down at the Stankovec refugee camps outside Skopje, Macedonia, attempting to understand the immensely complex aid need and network.

Standing on the border watching the line of refugees snaking back into the Kosovo hills from the Macedonian checkpoint, it was clear to me that we were witnessing a lucky escape; that is, if the stories were true that most Albanians had survived. It was not the sort of terrain you send a small group of soldiers into to take the country. It is beautiful, rolling countryside, which in places is quite mountainous. There was virtually nowhere for advancing troops to hide and plenty of vantage points for defending forces. Bill Clinton and Tony Blair seemed quite proud of their stouthearted defense of the Kosovar Albanians. There was good reason to be proud on one level, as their efforts compared very favorably with many countries that did not assist in the conflict at all. But it was also clear to even the most ignorant military strategist that if Slobodan Milosevic's "final solution" (as his policy was described) was anything other than

~~Never Again!~~ Yet Again!

pushing the Albanians over the border, then there would have been one more genocide in the twentieth century that left us standing. Fortunately for the victims, that was not his intent. Or if it was, it was never implemented. The brutality of their eviction, the organization of his troops, and the determination of his policy should have rung the loudest alarm bells that the Pentagon and Whitehall had available. There was a political and military reaction eventually, but not before hundreds of thousands of people were displaced. Thankfully, the majority were ultimately able to make their way home, however tragic the homecoming was in many cases.

Genocide did not occur in Kosovo. However, this crime against humanity that we witnessed was a long way down the pathway to genocide. NATO intervention eventually reversed the ethnic cleansing, but preventative policy had still failed again. We met refugees who had packed their bags months before the crisis. They knew it was just a matter of time before they would be expelled from their homes. Observers on the ground knew it. The problem was not that early warning did not provide sufficient information, but that the information was not processed in the right way, through channels that could make a difference to prevent mass atrocities or protect those at risk. The only reason that the Kosovar Albanians are still alive is because Mr. Milosevic did not kill them; not because we saved them. This time, James and I understood this more intimately, because we were seeing it with our own eyes and hearing it with our own ears.

The experience of being so close to the action influenced our thinking deeply. We decided that we needed to create a vehicle for predicting the development of genocide, and to mitigate its effects much earlier than the ineffectual scramble in Kosovo. We knew that we had let those people down, even though they didn't seem to realize it as they waved their "Thanks NATO!" flags. Before the outbreak of the crisis, we had been planning the extension of our work through the creation of the Aegis Trust, a new organization that we envisaged would work alongside the Holocaust Centre and assist the implementation of the "lessons

What Next?

of the Holocaust" in practice. We envisioned that Aegis (which means "protection") should address the fundamental issues within society that allow the fault lines to appear, which then facilitate the onset of the environment in which genocidal ideas can grow and succeed. Then, as we looked at the crisis in Kosovo, we decided that we should press ahead with the Aegis project in order to focus on strategies for the prevention of genocide.

Aegis Trust came formally into being in 2000, with the aim of bringing together a wide spectrum of scholars, journalists, nongovernmental organizations, governmental departments, and international organizations in order to assess how such a cross-sector group could best facilitate the implementation of preventative strategies. The aim was to help bridge the gap between the important academic research about genocide and policies that may prevent it. We were aware from the outset that this was a task too large for any one organization, but one that needed to be shared across a wide and talented group. We found ourselves supported by respected scholars of the Holocaust with serious intentions in supporting our goals. John Roth, then of Claremont McKenna College, California; Hubert Locke from Washington State University; Carol Rittner, from Richard Stockton College, New Jersey; Elisabeth Maxwell, founder of Remembering for the Future; and Richard L. Rubenstein of the University of Bridgeport, Connecticut, were the members of our initial executive. These scholars alone had over a hundred twenty years of teaching and researching about the Holocaust between them collectively! Along with that, they also had a real desire to see its implications taken seriously in the prevention of future genocide, and the impact of their work was significant. From this initial group of trusted friends, the development of a serious and committed network of prevention specialists has come into being, which provides a platform for changing the environment for preventative policy.

In January 2002, Aegis held the first cross-sector conference on the prevention of genocide, in which academics, government departments, military personnel, journalists, and nongovernmental

~~Never Again!~~ Yet Again!

organizations discussed the real possibilities of moving strategies forward in a meaningful way. The gathering was a joint project with the UK Foreign and Commonwealth Office, who saw the need to engage the debate as a policy issue. Working on behalf of ministers, the War Crimes Section showed the kind of vision necessary in foreign policy making to create important links between past events and future preventative policy. Convening such a conference, which may evoke direct criticism of the government that funded it, is courageous. It became ever more clear that making these changes was – and is – going to be hard work, because political will is associated with national interest, and if the interest of the country is at stake, or not promoted, then it is going to be difficult to convince decision makers to commit to providing resources to prevent the buildup of genocidal ideology. This is the real point. It takes both political will and financial resources to make early prevention possible. If we do not act early, then we gamble with people's lives as we did in Bosnia, Rwanda, and Kosovo. We have learned that when you gamble, sometimes you win and sometimes you lose. We cannot afford to gamble because we cannot lose, as the results are truly catastrophic.

Reducing risk means being committed to the cause of humanity and being altruistic in our foreign policy. When British Foreign Secretary Robin Cook talked about an "ethical foreign policy," some people laughed. The very thought of an ethical foreign policy was almost comical. The papers, the pundits, and the cynics knew it was impossible to achieve. Regrettably, they were right, but Cook was not wrong to try to reform foreign affairs from national interest to human interest. If the system does not allow the electorate that latitude, being clear about the demands we place upon our politicians is the first step. One of the biggest dangers of democracy is that it is self-serving. That is, the first priority of the voter – myself included – is to choose a party that most suits my own personal needs and interests. Therefore, politicians address those needs as they perceive them to be – or as the focus groups tell them. Health, education, crime, and economic stability are usually the issues of

WHAT NEXT?

any nation's well-being. But how many people actually vote based on a candidate's human rights agenda? How many parties would even think to include their conflict prevention or international aid policy in the manifesto or promotional material that drops onto your doormat? Have you ever seen that?

The original plan was for Aegis to be a policy think-tank group on genocide prevention, with a campaigning edge. However, we soon realized that in order to make changes to the way governments respond to the threat of genocide, it is also important to inform the public through the use of mass media and more formal education. Aegis soon became more closely associated with the day-to-day work of the Holocaust Centre, in attempting to highlight the need to understand the path to genocide with the visitors to the Centre. We had initially attempted to keep the two organizations distinct from each other, but there is a natural synergy. In teaching about the Holocaust, we introduce a moral imperative to be active in defending the rights of the vulnerable, identifying ideological hatred and violence, and rooting it out, wherever it might be. In this regard, Aegis is the perfect and natural partner for the Centre – and other Holocaust centers like it. It has a vital message that can apply in a number of educational and practical settings.

The partnership between Aegis and the Holocaust Centre has resulted in significant synergy. Both organizations function at the Centre to produce educational materials, documentary films, academic publications, and internet-based resources about genocide, including the Holocaust. An effective communications team has developed, producing high-quality, challenging materials to reach wider audiences. With the growth of internet access and the ever-shrinking global environment, we need tools to reach a very far-flung range of people. Our message is just as pertinent in Asia as it is in South America, and as it is here in the UK. Genocide is a global issue. We all need to develop global reach with our message.

Anyone involved in teaching about the Holocaust wants to make a difference to the world in which we live. That is presumably

~~Never Again!~~ Yet Again!

why we do what we do. How to balance the need to explain the specific experience of the Holocaust with the equally important need to find practical applications across a range of circumstances that raise similar issues is more complex.

In the world of Holocaust education and scholarship, as well as among survivors and their families, there are many fears that genocide issues might dilute the message of the Holocaust. Those fears are well founded as there are many, particularly on the left of the political spectrum, who would prefer to avoid a frank confrontation with the Holocaust and equivocate it with the general area of human rights. Such relativization cannot be justified on a whole range of levels. The Holocaust was unprecedented and horrifying in its scale and implementation. That said, those who really understand the Holocaust for the unprecedented genocide it was have a duty to take its message forward. We who work in the field should, of all people, be prepared and more willing to confront hatred, fight for the human rights of those who are oppressed, and seek to help heal the pain of the survivors of more recent mass atrocities, ethnic cleansing, and genocide.

Over the last few years, there has been a growing awareness of the need to incorporate the challenge of genocide more broadly into the research that is being conducted into the Holocaust and its consequences. Increasingly, departments and centers that teach about the Holocaust have included "Holocaust and Genocide" in their titles. By way of example, the Remembering for the Future 2000 international conference, the brainchild of Elisabeth Maxwell, had "The Holocaust in an Age of Genocide" as its subtitle. It brought together in one forum both Holocaust and genocide scholars, who successfully contributed over 200 papers on facing the challenge of the Holocaust in an age in which genocide persists.

Building bridges between the impact of genocide on real people's lives and our own cosseted existence is a task that takes concerted effort. Everyone needs to participate in this, across the spectrum of our society. In the United Kingdom and in the USA, there are now many opportunities to bring people together to

What Next?

discuss and learn about the Holocaust and events that raise similar issues. The Holocaust Centre is part of a growing landscape of sites, museums, and educational programs dedicated to teaching about the Holocaust and ensuring that its memory and challenge stay in the public memory. In the UK, the Holocaust Memorial Day Trust, the Imperial War Museum's Holocaust exhibition, the London Institute of Education, the Anne Frank Trust, the London Jewish Cultural Centre, the Holocaust Educational Trust, the Jewish Museum, and the Association of Jewish Refugees all have active programs of education which contribute to British society's knowledge and confrontation with the past. Such groups should always be supportive of one another. In turn, organizations around the world need to join forces to complement each other and benefit from the growth in research and education, creating shared goals. We live in a global environment and our message is global. We have the tools, the need, and the will. So implementation is the obvious next step.

The biggest danger now, with all the work that is happening, is that the Holocaust becomes overexposed within British society, leading to saturation and its gradual normalization. The more exposed people are to its message, the more complacent they are likely to become. Unlike in former Nazi-occupied countries, the Holocaust is not embedded in the landscape of the English or North American countryside. There are not former camps or deportation sites in every county, or places that Grandma remembers on every street corner – thankfully. But this also means that this is not our history, not in the sense that the landscape is permanently scarred with its memory. There are many connections to the history of the Holocaust engendered through the role of Britain and America at that time, but it does not have the same historical, social, and cultural impact as it does in Europe. The way in which we choose to remember the Holocaust has to find its connections to our past. We, then, have to make the social, cultural, and ethical connections to its implications. Even though it will always be an overwhelming chapter in our

~~Never Again!~~ Yet Again!

history books, this is the only way it will have an enduring presence in our lives.

The Holocaust Centre, Beth Shalom, is just one organization working with this aim. It will continue to grow and have its independent life. As it does so, it becomes clear that the work needs many alliances to makes its message effective. Actually, it can only do its work in collaboration with many, many other people and organizations. The key is finding the people with whom to work – those who can share the mission.

Chapter Seventeen
The Journey

I was listening to Bela Rosenthal describe the experience of being a child in Theresienstadt (Terezin). She was a mere toddler at the time she was incarcerated there. The small number of tiny children who had been left behind in the ghetto were placed in a room with virtually no adult supervision, little food and no context in which to develop linguistic and social skills. Hanging between no life and certain death at some point, there was no way those children should have survived. When Bela and the children in that room were liberated, they were virtually wild. They had no recognizable language, and no social skills whatsoever. They were more or less animals.

Not far away in the same ghetto, Martin Stern and Steven Frank were both under ten years old when they were liberated. In their cases, there were adults around them to guide them through unthinkable circumstances. Nevertheless, young eyes had absorbed the deportations, felt the pang of starvation. They knew precisely what they were experiencing even as such young children.

As I watched my own children, Natalia, Stephanie, and Aaron, who were all aged between five and ten years old, I wondered what the appropriate time would be to introduce the Holocaust to them. In the UK school system, they first learn about the *Diary of Anne Frank* at around the age of eight, and then the *Kindertransports* at age nine, so pupils have some content quite early, even if they are not entirely sure about the context. My

~~Never Again!~~ Yet Again!

children have obviously been exposed to more about the Holocaust than most children of their age, so they are not a good case around which to build pedagogy, but it occurred to me that we certainly did need a new pedagogy. I thought it was time to find out what that pedagogy would look like for younger learners. I developed the brief for a new permanent exhibition at the Centre, *The Journey*. The plan was to create an exhibit without photos or text, but rather an experiential set of spaces in which the younger visitor could learn about the stages of the Holocaust, driven by each child's inquiry.

The Journey tells the story of a fictional character, Leo Stein. Leo is ten years old and lives in Berlin. He is keeping a diary, to which the visitors have access in each room. First we are on the street where Leo lives; we learn about refugees and where they come from, the variety of reasons why, and the fact that there are many refugees today. Leo appears on screen (in 1936) and introduces visitors to the current problem of the growing power of National Socialism and the impact it is having on the population. We then move to his apartment, where we can explore his toys, his parents' desk, the table laid for Shabbat, and the toy box belonging to Leo and his little sister Hannah. We find out about their lives.

Next, we are in Leo's classroom, where we learn all about antisemitism, marginalization, peer pressure, and the Hitler Youth. As the situation deteriorates, we are back out on the street at *Kristallnacht*. The situation is frightening, noisy, and violent. Leo is worried about his grandparents who live in the countryside, and the telephone wires have been cut. He wonders what will happen next. In the next room, we are in his father's tailor shop. It has been damaged, but thankfully, Leo's father has returned after being briefly arrested. We hear the parents discussing what to do next. Do they flee, stay, or hide? They discuss the options. One option is that they send Leo and Hannah away to safety to England on the *Kindertransport* trains. Leo's father makes a hiding place anyway, in case the Nazis return. The visitors have to find the hiding place. In there, they learn that during the war

The Journey

some parents did indeed send their children into hiding as they had no other option.

Leo's parents decide to send him alone on the *Kindertransport*. The visitors enter a train carriage and sit on the benches. As the countryside flashes past, they hear about his journey and his concerns about his sister, his parents, and the people who will receive him at the other end. We also learn that most children were not lucky enough to make journeys to safety, but rather were sent to the ghetto and on trains to unknown destinations – from which they did not return.

In the final room of the exhibition, we learn how the refugee children arrived in the UK, and how they found their new lives, new languages, foster parents, and friends. We also learn about the few children who survived, like Bela, Steven, and Martin, and how after their survival in Theresienstadt, they made it to England, and we hear about the kind of lives they have subsequently led.

Imagine it is Monday and the visitors are going around the exhibition. There are various touch screens around the exhibit where either the teacher or the children themselves can access short clips of testimony relevant to the themes in the room. Lisa Vincent was a Kindertransportee. We follow her story around the exhibit as we go. In the final room, Lisa, who volunteers for the Centre, is waiting to receive the children and answer their questions. Now imagine it is Tuesday and let's say Simon Winston, a hidden child during the Holocaust, is volunteering today. When the visitors go around the exhibit, they can access Simon's testimony clips, building a picture of his life story, before meeting him in the discussion forum. This way, any number of survivor volunteers can participate and the exhibition moulds to their stories.

The real question then was whether young people of nine to twelve years old would have the capacity and maturity to handle the material we were presenting. We needed to find out. Over a period of a year or so, we developed the concept of the museum and some of its content. We then worked with a small number of primary schools in Nottinghamshire and Lincolnshire to present

~~Never Again!~~ Yet Again!

the topics to the young people. We even used parts of the main historical exhibition to test their ability to work with historical material around the subject area. We also spent considerable time bringing the younger students and Holocaust survivors together in order to find out the levels of their inquiry.

What we discovered very quickly was that younger learners had tremendous capacity to inquire and to explore the boundaries of the experience. They were fearless in their line of questioning and while some of the questions lacked maturity, nevertheless it was clear that they were going to be able to manage a great deal of content. We decided to focus on principles. So we started with identity and family, with peer pressure and groups, with hatred and persecution, with choices and who made what choice to act in what way. We decided that topics such as the agonizing decision facing parents, and the consequences of actions and counter-actions were important points of access for the younger visitor. We decided to avoid role play in the traditional sense of taking on an actual character, but rather worked with understanding choices and scenarios, so that the young people would think about the options – or lack of options – available to the Jews in that situation.

It proved to be a very potent model for the age group. So, for example, when they process the difficult decision facing Leo's parents after *Kristallnacht*, they discuss issues such as what they would need to do to flee, what the consequences might be if they chose to stay, whether or not there was an option to hide or "disappear" within the society. As they work through the choices, they discover that leaving Nazi Germany was virtually impossible, and the dangers of trying were very high. They would need helpers; they would need to have papers; they would need to have support from overseas, maybe relatives in another country. As the list of obstacles increases and the threats equally so, it becomes plain to the children just how oppressive and impossible it was to live as Jews at that time. From that realization come the questions about what the options really were, about why other countries did not do something to rescue them. What kinds of people were needed to be able to help? Was there anything else

The Journey

the Jews could do? Why didn't local German neighbors help? The list of questions itself builds up a picture of what was possible and what was not.

The Journey has demonstrated that just as in math or English, the first principles can be put in place at a very young age. We are not expecting children of ten years old to have the maturity or analytical skill to decipher the Holocaust as a complex history. But we now know that with the right support, teaching environment, and stimulus material, they are just as capable of asking the fundamental questions with which we all struggle.

CHAPTER EIGHTEEN
A GIRL CALLED IRENE

The smell was distinct. It was the smell of lingering death. I had never smelled it before, but instinctively I knew. It seeped out through the cracks in the tin shed, permeated the air. It was not pungent, more insipid, hanging heavy on warm air. The tin gate creaked on its hinges, illuminating the dim room. Shafts of sun fell across rows of ivory spheres. I immediately noticed how they were neatly stacked. Someone had carefully placed the skulls there, lining them up, orderly in their disarray.

The image of shelves of thousands of skulls, in shed after shed, was going to become familiar. In Kigali, Ntarama, Nyamata, Bisesero, and other sites where Tutsis were murdered during the genocide in Rwanda, the remnants of destruction were stacked up. It was a stark reminder of just how recent this all was. It was the last days of 2001. Less than eight years after the genocide, and still death hung in the air. We closed the creaking door and moved to the next tin shed along. This time, there was no order; there were no neat lines of humanity stacked up. There was just a pile of rotting clothes entangled and heaped high under the tin structure. The tin walls were missing in places; clothes spilling out of the pole structure were entirely open to the elements. Someone had decided that these personal items from genocide victims should be retained and preserved for the record. Then they were left to rot outside. I was trying to make sense of this

~~Never Again!~~ Yet Again!

mass of wasted humanity, and then I realized that it was not the heap that mattered. I looked closer. I saw an orange sweater, a really pretty blouse too, and a child's shoe.

But I start in the wrong place.

The plane soared through cloudless skies above Kenya. The flat, browned landscape unfolded below; the shadow of the plane's vapor trail streaked a black line across the landscape of an African topography. Sunburned savannah stretched for mile after uninterrupted mile. I squinted vainly, hoping the mottled landscape was elephant herds, but suspected I was looking at the tops of occasional scattered trees in the orange dust. All of a sudden, the landscape reached up towards the plane, rising some 4,000 feet towards the clouds in a flourish of forest. Hills rolled into one another; rich, deep green countryside, curving, meandering over the horizon. Rwanda. That's the first thing you notice about Rwanda – its beauty, not the stench of death. Hills, forests, lakes, then more hills, and more forest. Rwanda really is a beautiful country. That vibrancy also translates into the people. Energy, color, drive, opportunity, expectancy – that's what one feels there.

Juxtaposed against that vibrancy and energy, the genocide of 1994 seems to be an aberration. It really does not square with what appears to be the placid nature of the people of Rwanda. And yet there are killers and their accomplices everywhere. So, too, there are the surviving victims and their traumatized pasts gliding like ghosts, nameless, shapeless, through the streets. Sometimes you can see these ghosts relatively easily – a missing limb, a slashed arm, a deeply scarred face. Other times you have to look more closely – dull eyes, a withered spirit, a wounded soul. But these only manifest themselves in moments when they let their guard down and let you see into their bleeding hearts.

In 2002, the people of Rwanda were uncertain what to do next about commemorating the genocide. They had already established a memorial period between April and July. These few months reflect the period in which the genocide took place in 1994. Survivors gathered on killing sites and kept vigil through the

A Girl Called Irene

night of April 7th, beside blazing bonfires, dark faces staring. Searing flames. Searing pain.

How does a country commemorate the genocide? It ripped through the communities, bringing the country to bleeding knees. There was nothing left, save the stench of death. Genocide in Rwanda happened everywhere. It took place street by street, house by house. Its hideous imprint was everywhere, literally everywhere. So destructive was the force of the wanton destruction of the *Interahamwe* – the Hutu militia – that the infrastructure of the country was in tatters. Homes were destroyed, communities scattered or decimated, and the biggest demographic change of Rwanda's history convulsed into effect. Almost a quarter of the total population was erased; killers fled, survivors fled, and a huge influx of returning Tutsi refugees from a generation earlier filled the yawning gaps. There were corpses buried in shallow graves, families buried in backyards, and an unidentified number of widows and orphans. HIV-infected rape victims had no support. The trauma was so deep that counseling services simply could not cope with demand. The problem was where to begin.

Some survivors of the Rwandan genocide had visited the Holocaust Centre. James met Ancilla Mukarubuga in London. She was representing the Rwandan widows' association, AVEGA, and he filmed her for a short documentary. When she heard about the Centre, she jumped on the train with James and took the ride north. Walking around the museum, she gasped when she saw the photographs depicting racial types: the "typical Aryan" and the "typical Jew." "This is what they did in our country, too. They categorized Hutus and Tutsis, made us different, better or worse, depending on how you looked." That racial typing began to cleave Rwandans apart – and then tear them apart. When Ancilla reached the ghetto exhibition and saw the images of bereft, doomed Jewish children, she reached into her purse and, with tears rolling down her cheeks, showed me faded color photographs of her own family murdered in the genocide a few years earlier. It was no longer a tale in far-off

~~Never Again!~~ Yet Again!

Africa, with statistics and dates. Genocide in Rwanda was about people with names and homes. It was about this woman of my own age, standing in the Holocaust Centre weeping for her children.

During 2000 and 2001, we received several faxes from Rwanda's minister of youth, sport and culture, asking us to consider being involved in resolving some of the post-genocide commemoration issues. We politely declined because we thought it was beyond our competency and capacity. Then, in late 2001, James attended a conference in Kigali convened by Yael Danieli, a psychologist with a deep interest in post-genocide trauma. Along with Ibuka – the survivors' organization in Rwanda – and victims of a number of genocides, the conference addressed the issues of survival and national healing. I took a call from James during the conference, in which he ordered me to get on a plane to Rwanda as soon as possible. Three weeks later, I was flying over the East African savannah, wondering what I was about to encounter.

The survivors of the genocide knew it was important to have recognition and voice. The Rwandan government knew it was important to preserve the memory of the genocide. The local populace could not avoid commemorating the past as each year there was an official day of memory and mourning, with morning until evening coverage on all broadcast channels. But how to provide the right process for preserving the remnants of destruction, how to structure a meaningful narrative, how to create the right kind of spaces for public reflection and recognition, this was an altogether different matter.

James and I spent two weeks traveling the country, visiting sites of the genocide, meeting survivors, trying to understand the geography, topography, and narrative of the genocide. It was more challenging than I had imagined. With very few written sources and no clear iconic images, imagining the genocide was extremely difficult. I interviewed several genocide survivors. We took with us Apollon Kabahizi, whose family had been caught up in the genocide. Apollon had been in the Rwandan Patriotic

A Girl Called Irene

Front, one of the liberators of Kigali under the stunning military brilliance of Paul Kagame. Many of Kabahizi's family had been murdered. Three siblings – Emanuel, Romain, and Pothin – had survived the killings in their own suburb of Kigali. In their family's history, there were so many elements of the genocide as a whole. Claire, his sister, had fled to Burundi, then beyond. Emanuel was on the run, hiding, getting caught, hiding again; the home was destroyed, the parents killed; he was trapped in the UN compound and only escaped on the day the UN fled – along with Romain, one of very few survivors of the ETO school at Kicukiro. Apollon was one of the liberators, holding a mortar position not more than a mile from where his family was being murdered.

We then created a traveling exhibition in England called *100 Nights*. We integrated the experiences of the Kabahizi family into the exhibit to demonstrate how the genocide affected just a single family in so many different ways. Seven years after the genocide, Apollon and his siblings had discovered the desiccated corpses of his pregnant sister and brother-in-law. They were to bury them at a site of mass burial at Gisozi, a suburb of Kigali.

The site at Gisozi was a mixture of total misery and an odd sense of hope. The tin sheds with the skulls, shown first on the BBC by veteran Rwanda correspondent Fergal Keane, were a shocking introduction to the genocide. I did not learn about the genocide by being in Rwanda during the genocide itself, but I certainly got a better sense of it in those horrendous tin sarcophagi to mass killing at Gisozi and other sites. As you look at a single skull, with the machete cut clearly visible in the top portion of the bone, it leaves you with plenty to think about. And then when you look at the tiny skull next to it, with the laceration on the top portion of the skull, front to back, no forensic or anatomical training is required. It is the skull of a child running away when he or she was struck.

We also made a fifteen-minute film, *Secrets of a Thousand Hills*, documenting some of the genocide sites, and our reaction to them.

~~Never Again!~~ Yet Again!

It takes a while for the full impact of the genocide in Rwanda to sink in. Today, the same streets where the gangs of militia roamed around are vibrant by day, quiet by night. But in those very streets, on virtually every intersection, killers had lurked, trying to catch Tutsis in their tightening net. I have often had people explain to me that what happened in Rwanda was an example of tribal warfare. I am not sure what image that is supposed to conjure up – possibly the idea of wild bushmen living primitive lives, who just could not help but kill the "other" in spontaneous violence. Nothing could be further from the truth. Rwanda certainly did have tribes, but it is clear that genocide was organized centrally and delivered locally. There was a clear chain of command and a clear structure for delivery of the genocidal plan. There was nothing spontaneous about it at all.

The genocide in Rwanda was a legacy of European influence in that tiny East African country. During the period when the Germans ran the territory (1895–1916), Rwandans were already being studied by the same race scientists whose ideas helped justify National Socialism. Then, during the time of the Belgian colonists, the population was fixed into Hutus and Tutsis to assist with the administration of the country. The Belgians needed a managerial class. There was a broad distinction, although not strictly adhered to by any means: the Hutus worked the land and the Tutsis kept cattle. The Belgians used this general rule of thumb. Until then, it had been possible to move from one group to another, but under colonial rule, ethnicity not only became fixed – it determined a person's opportunities. If an individual had more than five cows, he or she was classed as Tutsi. The Tutsis became the colonists' de facto managers – a smaller group of people, who were controllable and able to administer on their behalf.

Not long before the Belgians handed back Rwanda's independence, they realized the folly of their decision. It was clear that there was resentment among the Hutus and they feared there would be a backlash when they left. And so they reversed their policy on military conscription and almost overnight turned the

A Girl Called Irene

army into a trained Hutu fighting force. In effect, they armed the backlash. On their departure, the Hutus, who had been angry about the oppression under the Belgians, lashed out at the Tutsis in a violent, staged uprising in 1959.

Many Tutsis fled in the ten years that followed, as one after another, waves of violence were visited upon them. Tens of thousands of Tutsis were killed and many more fled the country prior to the genocide in 1994. I interviewed many people about the genocide. In each interview, I always asked the question, "When did the genocide begin?" Not one survivor answered the question as being 1994. Most argue that genocide began in 1959. The Tutsi victims knew that they were being targeted in a concerted effort long before the killing spree of 1994 erupted. Occasional reports of the killings and persecution hit the Western media. The road that ended in the most brutal mass murder since the Holocaust had two generations of warnings that went unheeded.

The genocide in Rwanda was one of the greatest travesties of the twentieth century. It was a double-edged sword, too, a dangerous conspiracy of outright evil and willful inaction. This was not an event enacted a generation before my birth. This time, I was a twenty-seven-year-old voting member of the British public, who, like many, sat in front of the television and watched it unfold before my very eyes – and still did nothing. The perpetrators were clearly the Hutu Power regime and their organized network of militia, who slaughtered the best part of a million people in twelve weeks. But it was not possible without the connivance of the UN, which withdrew its activities in the country after the killing began. Reinforcements would have prevented the genocide, as General Romeo Dallaire, the very capable leader of peacekeeping operations, made clear to his colleagues in New York. But around the Security Council table, there was no intention to risk the lives of UN soldiers. And so women and children died instead – and in infinitely larger numbers. In January 2002, Aegis inaugurated its international award "For Altruism, Resourcefulness and Bravery in Preserving the Value of

~~Never Again!~~ Yet Again!

Human Life," which was presented to Romeo Dallaire. Although his mission failed to prevent or end the genocide, it was not without a tremendously courageous effort on his part, and thousands of Tutsis – the ethnic group targeted for killing – do owe their lives to his efforts and those of others like him. In presenting the award to Dallaire, Foreign Office Minister Peter Hain stated, "General Dallaire, as commander of the UN Assistance Mission, found his warnings of impending calamity discounted and disregarded by his superiors in the governments – including that, I am sorry to say, of the United Kingdom – to which they were reported. The tragic consequences have left a stain on the collective conscience of the world. We failed to prevent genocide." That the Foreign and Commonwealth Office recognizes this need for change should give us all a degree of hope in the face of future conflicts. However, the resolve will only be known when it is put to the test.

By the spring of 2002, between us we had made several trips to Rwanda. Then Aloisea Inyumba visited the Holocaust Centre. She headed up the Rwandan National Unity and Reconciliation Commission and had been with me at the second Stockholm Forum, with the Rwandan delegation. On her way home, she came via England to see us. Her soft voice and slight frame belied the enormity of the challenge she faced with the commission, and the toughness with which she went about her work. She was taking up a new position as governor of Rural Kigali Province and wanted us to work with her. She insisted we go back to Rwanda to do something concrete there.

James and I discussed the possibility that we could help the government to develop a small genocide memorial in Aloisea's province, somewhere out of sight of the public eye. If survivors welcomed it and it had useful education outputs, perhaps it could become a model of good practice.

James decided to commit more time to Rwanda. He spent the best part of the next three years there. He stopped his part-time medical career completely to establish Aegis Rwanda. Initially, his main objective was to seek the opinion of survivors and others in the community and the Rwandan government about the future of genocide memory, in particular the sites of genocide and how that memory might impact on the next generation.

He had been invited to dinner by Dick Goldman, head of US Agency for International Development, as part of these discussions. At the end of the evening, they viewed our short film, *Secrets of a Thousand Hills*. The memorial at Gisozi featured in the film; a quarter of a million victims of the genocide were buried there. The Kigali City Council had erected a building – still a shell at the time, but filled with shelves stacked with human remains. In the film, we asked the question, what form would memory take at such a place in the future? Our question lay somewhere between the philosophical and rhetorical. That was, until Théoneste walked in.

Théoneste Mutsindashyaka is a cheerful and decisive man. Dark-skinned, bright-eyed, he flashes a smile and oozes confidence. He was the mayor of Kigali City. Being late was his trademark. He walked in after dinner had ended, just as the film was being screened. James called me that evening, saying that the mayor was being persuasive, insistent; he wanted Aegis to work with him to develop Gisozi. It was a major project and carried all kinds of risks. James was firm down the crackly phone line. "Our board won't like it, but I think we should give the mayor a hearing."

A few weeks later, we sat late one night as Théoneste explained that the mass burial site in the heart of the city of Kigali needed shape and form. He explained that he had hoped that in the same way as Yad Vashem or the United States Holocaust Museum told the history of the Holocaust, one day on the site at Gisozi, people would come to remember and to learn. He was serious, focused, determined. There had been plans to put up a building on the site, in which the bones in the tin sheds would be displayed in an ossuary, with some kind of exhibition explaining why they were installed there. The building had been designed and was halfway up when work was halted. Mutsindashyaka realized it needed further thought and more money.

We were down at the site the next day. The tin sheds with the skulls and bones and personal effects clung to the hillside low

~~Never Again!~~ Yet Again!

down. Further up the slope, a terrace had been made, where five mass graves had been created. These were large concrete boxes where survivors and their families could come and bury their loved ones at a single site, under the auspices of Ibuka. The Rwandan authorities had first used the site to take corpses from the city streets and bury them safely in one place to avoid an epidemic. The site was never a killing center, but rather a collecting point for human remains. The city council, headed by the mayor's office, also realized that since the genocide had taken place all over the city, there would be graves and human remains everywhere. For practical reasons, they determined that it was more appropriate to have a single site of remembrance and reflection for the city, rather than hundreds of small sites depicting the mass destruction on every street corner.

We were asked if we would be able to come up with a plan to raise the money to complete the construction of the building, to design its contents, and develop a meaningful education program. In short, Mutsindashyaka wanted us to create a memorial museum similar to the one we had built in England, and to make it reality in less than two years, for the tenth anniversary of the genocide. It was a tall order. The money was not in place; the building was a half-complete concrete shell; there was no design brief; there had been no stakeholder discussions; there was no real sense at that point as to what it should achieve. In fact, there were even more fundamental principles at stake that we needed to discuss.

There were questions about whether it was appropriate, eight years after the genocide, to create a public space. The trauma was still very raw; the society was very fragile; the justice process was underway, but nowhere near complete. There were concerns that a public center would attract unwanted attention, that it would be divisive for the society, that its presence would be resented by the Hutu majority, and that there would be some kind of kick-back against the project, or worse – that it would engender division and unrest in an already fragile society. This is a danger and remains so, but collective memory happens anyway. It is better to try to shape the memory than to allow it to fester.

A Girl Called Irene

When the ministry of youth, sports and culture had first invited us, our response was, "Who do we think we are to be advising on genocide memory in Rwanda?" Our next thought was that developing memorials and a genocide education program in Rwanda was all too early.

"The question is," James said, "when will it be too late?" Survivors were clearly attempting to tell their story and remind the world for a reason. In two years' time, attention would focus on Rwanda for the tenth anniversary of the genocide. "How will survivors feel if the remains of their loved ones are still scattered on the floors of churches and no one appears to be listening?" Publicly acknowledging pain, loss, and failure is part of reparation, healing, and rebuilding. We concluded that the tenth anniversary of the genocide must provide a positive signal for survivors that the world is responding to them, not an affirmation that few people really care.

There was also concern about raising and spending $2million on a memorial center at a time when many genocide survivors were close to starvation, and HIV/AIDS victims of genocidal rape could not afford the anti-retroviral medication and were on the point of death. James and his team undertook a series of stakeholder discussions with community leaders, grassroots leadership at local level, and with genocide survivors. It was overwhelmingly accepted that creating a permanent memorial in the heart of the capital city was the right thing to do. Lay leaders of all backgrounds understood and supported it. Genocide survivors understood that poverty and AIDS would always be a problem, but that it should not deter the project to create the memorial, which they wholeheartedly endorsed.

It then came down to the concept and money. James led Aegis Rwanda – and still does. I was appointed project director with a mission to ensure that the permanent exhibition was ready for Kigali Memorial Centre to open in April 2004. A board was established to represent the Kigali City Council, the owners of the site. It was a lay board of Kigali city officials, members of civil society, including survivors, and chaired by

~~Never Again!~~ Yet Again!

Suzanne Ruboneka and the Member of Parliament, the Honorable Evariste Kalisa.

An executive committee was also formed for the duration of the project. This was essentially a design board, which met to discuss the Centre's content and assist with supporting its success at a senior level. Its members were mainly cabinet ministers, the chair of Ibuka, and the Aegis team.

I set to work with my team to look at the design of the Centre. We conceived a place that was dignified and reflective, a place principally for the surviving family members. We wanted a place of quietness where the restless victims could be at some kind of peace, their wasteful and tragic fates recognized fully through the peace and beauty of the Centre. And so we planned a memorial garden with our very able gardener Aime Le Grande. We wanted to surround the hideous concrete sarcophagi with the beauty of the gardens, and to create a place where survivors and their families could reflect in peaceful surroundings.

We planned a historical museum, telling the story of the genocide by tracing its convoluted path from the early twentieth century all the way through to the post-genocide issues of the early twenty-first century. We knew that telling the story was important not only for the wider world, but also for Rwanda itself. A generation was growing up that did not remember the genocide and yet was subject to its consequences. There were many even of Tutsi background who had returned to the country and needed to know what had happened, because it had not been their experience. It was only eight years on, but it was very clear that the country needed to know, because already there was ignorance and denial.

James worked with the mayor and city council to mobilize funds, but it was not easy. Many international donors stated that it was time for Rwanda to "move on" and could not understand that the memorial looked forward as well as back. Eventually, Bill Clinton pledged the first donation. The Swedish and Belgian governments followed, but the funds were only in sight four months before the opening was due in April 2004 to mark the tenth anniversary of the genocide.

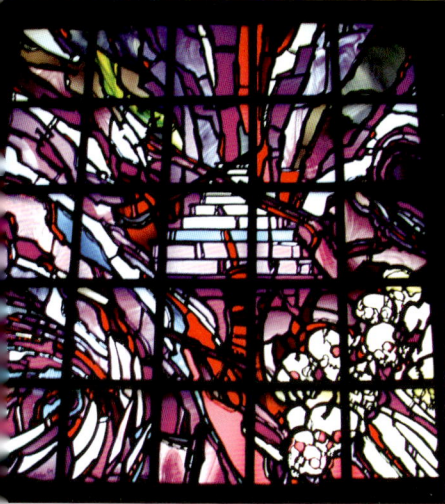

Top left: One of two stained-glass windows at the Kigali Genocide Memorial Centre, created by Ardyn Halter

Top right: The then mayor of Kigali, Théoneste Mutsindashyaka

Right: Memorial gardens freshly planted at the Kigali Genocide Memorial Centre, 2004

Photographs of genocide victims at the Kigali Centre are not placed behind glass, but left open for visitors to hold and examine; survivors continuously add images of their loved ones to this growing memorial

Top: The then US president George W. Bush and First Lady Laura Bush visit the Kigali Genocide Memorial Centre, February 2008

Right: James in conversation at the Kigali Centre with the then US secretary of state, Condoleezza Rice, February 2008

President Bill Clinton on one of several visits to the Kigali Centre

Top: Former British prime minister Tony Blair lays a wreath on mass graves at the Kigali Genocide Memorial Centre

Left: Meeting Rwanda's president, Paul Kagame, at the Centre

UN secretary-general Ban Ki Moon lays a wreath on mass graves at the Kigali Centre, in which over 250,000 victims of the 1994 genocide lie buried

Top: Irene Umutoni; a daddy's girl who loved fresh fruit and whose favorite toy was a doll she shared with her sister. The girls were together in the shower when a grenade was thrown in, killing them both. The discovery of Irene's story was to shape the children's memorial at the Kigali Genocide Memorial Centre (right).

Fabrice Murenzi Minega. Age: 8. Favorite sport: swimming. Favorite sweets: chocolate. Best friend: his mom. Behavior: gregarious. Cause of death: bludgeoned with a club.

Top: When James visited the Chad-Sudan border in 2004, he met Fatima, who had been widowed, gang-raped and was pregnant as a result. Mass rape was a marked feature of the violence in Darfur.

On September 17, 2006, the first global Day for Darfur took place, with rallies in dozens of capital cities around the world calling for the protection of Darfur's African population. Here, thousands of demonstrators throng the street outside the Sudanese Embassy in London.

Held in May 2005, Aegis' "Protect Darfur" rally in Whitehall, central London, was one of the first major demonstrations on the Darfur crisis. Here Holocaust survivor John Fransman addresses the crowd.

Top: Mukesh Kapila (center) with James and the leadership of Aegis Students, following his keynote speech to their annual conference at the Holocaust Centre, September 2009. As head of the UN in Sudan in 2004, Kapila blew the whistle on the Darfur crisis.

Left: Halima, 13, saw her twin shot in the head during the Janjaweed attack that left her with a shattered left arm. Photographed by James on the Chad-Sudan border, along with thousands of other desperate refugees from Darfur, seen lining up for food aid (below).

Primary schoolchildren listen to a survivor at the Holocaust Centre. The Journey exhibition, opened in 2008, is designed to help younger children learn about some of the issues raised by the Holocaust.

Visitors to The Journey *travel back in time to Germany, 1938, arriving first in the living room of Leo Stein, the boy whose journey they will follow. They visit Leo's classroom, street, his father's tailor's shop, and the family hiding space and then get into the train carriage, arriving eventually in refuge in England. The exhibition is intentionally tactile, allowing youngsters wherever possible to handle historical items or replicas.*

A Girl Called Irene

Théoneste wanted to have a memorial dedicated to the children who were murdered. He had seen "Daniel's Story," the exhibit at the United States Holocaust Memorial Museum designed for younger visitors. He said he wanted "something similar." He also wanted it when the Centre opened, which was only a few months away. It was a tall order, but I put my mind to it. I had many ideas, but none of them quite worked. I decided I would come back to it, because we were just starting a project to collect as much information from around Kigali as we could find. Over fifty data gatherers had been trained, and they were going to go street by street, house by house in search of memories, documents, photographs and artifacts. It was a big job.

It was 8:30 in the morning. I had just made coffee and had sat down behind my desk. The previous day had been the first day of the data collection project. One of the team came to my desk. He was carrying a brown envelope. Without saying much, he tipped the contents onto my desk. There were various bits of paper, mainly documents and a letter. But among them were also a number of photos. As the pile spread out on my desk, on top was a photograph of a small girl. She had big eyes and was excited by the camera that had captured her. She did not appear to be more than four years old. "What a beautiful child!" I exclaimed. "Who is she?" "She was killed," came the blunt reply.

There was a silence as I took that fact in. "She was killed by a grenade in the shower." I stopped dead. There was total silence as I held the photo, my hands shaking. I thought of my own children, Natalia, Stephanie, and Aaron, who were three, five, and six years old. I wondered how similar she might have been to them. I wondered what kind of person she had been. I didn't like her being defined by the way she was brutally murdered. "What else do we know about her? What was her favorite food? What were her favorite toys? What were her first words?" My colleague looked at me blankly. "I don't know." Of course he didn't, but he looked at me as though he should know those things. "Who gave you the photo?" I asked. "Her uncle. He also told us that she and

~~Never Again!~~ Yet Again!

her sister were drowned in scalding water." I asked him to return to see the uncle and come back the next day.

The next day, I learned that Irene was six years old; that her favorite toy was a doll she shared with her sister; that she loved fresh fruit and was a "daddy's girl"; that she had died in the shower with her sister after a grenade was thrown in.

In the meantime, I had found another picture of a boy called Fabrice pulling a happy face in front of a Christmas tree. I wanted to know more about him, too. As these children came alive, their deaths became even more poignant. Cutting. Wrenching.

Getting to know a girl called Irene became the defining moment of my time in Rwanda. Her life spoke to me and the cruelty and devastation of her death will never leave me. As I sat and looked at their faces, children just like my own came into being. I knew I wanted others to know them that way, too. I decided not to create a fictional narrative about children during the genocide, but just to present their photos and their lives, using daylight to backlight huge photos and including a brief biography of their defining characteristics. Fabrice's reads:

Fabrice MURINZI MINEGA
Age: 8

Favorite sport: Swimming
Favorite sweets: Chocolate
Best friend: His mom
Behavior: Gregarious
Cause of death: Bludgeoned with a club

The picture of Irene was not the only moment of realization. We eventually reached a decision, in discussion with the survivors and Ibuka, that we would bury most of the human remains. A small collection was to be displayed in the exhibit in smoked-glass cases. The rest would be buried in the mass graves. But there was a terrible task still to be done. There was a room containing the contents of several mass graves that had been exhumed. Bone fragments, clothes, shoes, personal effects. At some point, we would have to go through the heap. It was kept in a concrete store room with the door locked. We took a box of rubber gloves and aprons and went in, to sift the mound of death. We knew that most of the pile would be buried in coffins at a special ceremony at the tenth anniversary. But first, we wanted to see if there were any items that were helpful to the historical record. The stench in that room is still printed onto my nasal lining. Suffocating with the effects of heat and human dust, we painstakingly sifted the remains. A cardigan, a shoe, an identity card, a comb, a child's pelvis, a sock. On and on, there seemed no end. We worked quickly but carefully, placing most of the contents of the heap into the coffins we had brought in. At the end of the horrible day's work, there was a stack of coffins and several trays of items which the victims had taken to their untimely graves.

The Memorial Centre had to maintain a delicate balance of roles. For the survivors, it was a place of mourning and memory. Frequent funerals at the side of the mass graves meant that families from around Kigali were committing their families into permanent memory there. For young people, the Centre was to be a place of learning, with a full education program planned on the site, using the exhibition and gardens. For the general public, the exhibition was there to inform, and the gardens to provide a place of reflection. For historians, the Centre's commitment to participate in creating a national archive of the genocide would contribute to knowledge. For the international community, it was to be a place of warning.

Five years later, in 2009, aside from being a dignified resting place for commemoration, the Kigali Genocide Memorial Centre has three programs. Firstly, genocide education: each day some sixty high-school students, children of survivors and children of perpetrators, learn together about the lessons of genocide, including about individual responsibility to prevent such crimes. Secondly, the documentation project is working with partners, including the University of Texas and USC Shoah Foundation Institute, to ensure that the testimonies and other important archives are preserved and made accessible for the world. This

~~Never Again!~~ Yet Again!

should form the basis of a national genocide archive. Finally, vulnerable survivors are supported through Aegis Rwanda's social program, including by creating jobs to help lift them out of destitution.

In summary, over the last eight years we have been working with colleagues and survivors of the genocide in Rwanda to see how best to tell the story of that genocide, and assist in drawing the necessary conclusions from it. We work with many survivors of the genocide. An amazing number of them are incredibly resourceful and have created new lives out of nothing. Others have been left without their families, without their children, without a home, without employment, or they may be dying from HIV/AIDS as a result of the gang rapes during the genocide. Time and time again, James has expressed his anger and frustration that once more, a vulnerable group of people who need to be heard and understood are left to suffer in silence.

The story of the creation of Kigali Memorial Centre will be the subject of another book, so numerous are the issues that it raises. Aside from serving survivors and young Rwandans, international visitors flock to the Kigali Genocide Memorial. George W. Bush, Condoleezza Rice, Tony Blair, and David Cameron are among the many world leaders who not only pay respects to the victims, but are reminded of the consequences when people in their position fail to uphold their obligations to protect people from genocide.

Ban Ki-Moon, secretary-general of the United Nations, contributed $10,000 from his own funds towards survivors. He reflected after his visit:

> In the memorial book I wrote, "Never, ever again, in the name of humanity, should we repeat this tragedy." Words fail to describe what I was thinking. I was crying myself.
>
> I couldn't express how horrified, how much sorrow I felt over what I had seen, for all those victims and families. It made me resolve, once again, that, as secretary-general, I should do all in my power to prevent such a tragedy in the name of humanity.

A Girl Called Irene

But this Memorial is not simply a register of atrocities. It is also a repository of hope. It is a call to never forget, and today I say loud and clear: NEVER AGAIN.

This memorial is also a call to justice. Justice will not heal all wounds, but putting an end to impunity can ensure that our cry of NEVER AGAIN will become an enduring reality, not only in Rwanda but for our common humanity.

CHAPTER NINETEEN

~~NEVER AGAIN!~~ YET AGAIN!

It seemed to be happening all over again. We were right in the middle of building a memorial as a warning from history, this time in Rwanda, when genocide recurred.

At the end of March 2004, we were working feverishly to complete the Kigali Genocide Memorial in time to be opened when heads of state and VIPs would fly in on April 7th, the tenth anniversary of the genocide. Several hundred laborers were carrying bricks and cement, digging trenches, and building walls. We had exhibition fitters from England; artist Ardyn Halter, the son of Holocaust survivors Roman and Susie Halter, was waiting to fit his spectacular stained glass windows. The documentation team was still out filming testimonies for the exhibition and the exhibit was still being proofread in England. I flew back to England to make sure it got on the plane, and dealt with hundreds of last-minute adjustments and corrections. There were sixty tons of material, in three languages, from a good number of different suppliers, to coordinate, pack, and ship. There were reports to make, generators to fix, donors to talk to, ambassadors to meet and ministers to brief. The Aegis team was also involved in organizing the tenth anniversary events to be held in the national stadium. Our friend Martin Hutchinson flew in as the artistic director of the ceremony. He wanted to know the budget for the international ceremony that was just six weeks away. There was no budget.

~~Never Again!~~ Yet Again!

So it was from January to April 2004: late nights, early mornings, endless coordination, and meetings with the team.

In the middle of all this, news started to trickle out about Darfur in Western Sudan.

The head of the United Nations in Sudan, Mukesh Kapila, had been interviewed on the BBC and spoke about the world's worst humanitarian crisis. The thrust of his message was that, "The only difference between Darfur and Rwanda is the speed and the timing. It is taking longer to kill people in Darfur, but what is happening is the same." He also made it clear that in his view the government of Sudan was responsible for these grievous crimes against humanity.

The timing resonated with us. Ten years after the Rwandan genocide, world leaders were reflecting on the lessons learned. Overlooking genocide and failing to prevent it is one thing, but doing so while discussing past failures would be like a fire brigade not attending an emergency because they had a fire drill. For Aegis Trust, ignoring a threat of genocide while opening another memorial would have been shameful.

We recalled the same situation in 1994, when we were building the Holocaust Centre while missing the genocide in Rwanda. We remembered our desperation to do something about Srebrenica when Bosnian Muslims were shot into mass graves in Europe. But we had neither the knowledge nor the connections at the time to say anything meaningful, and did not know who to turn to. That was why Aegis had been established – to respond to just such an event, to build competence and knowledge, political and media connections – and to give a credible, respected voice to victims of genocide, who are so often ignored.

The problem for governments and analysts – and indeed for organizations like Aegis Trust – is knowing when to respond, and to which threats. Darfur was not the only report of pending atrocities in March 2004. North of Rwanda, the Lord's Resistance Army in Northern Uganda was committing unimaginable, brutal crimes against children and women, and in Eastern Congo killings of civilians had become routine. Neither of these was

~~Never Again!~~ Yet Again!

genocide as had occurred in Rwanda or in the Holocaust, but every week it seems there is another report about a threat of conflict or possible genocide somewhere in the world. It is impossible to respond to everything all the time. The media and politicians grow fatigued with one tragedy, never mind multiple crises. If we make a noise about genocide each time there is a report or threat, very soon no one will listen anymore.

The policy team decided that Aegis should focus on one crisis where we might be able to make a tangible difference. In 2004, the looming crisis was in Darfur.

I continued to work on the detail of the museum in Kigali. James stayed in Rwanda until the opening of the Kigali Memorial Centre, then headed out to Darfur via Chad, where the refugees were reported to be heading.

While still in Rwanda, James spoke with the small Aegis policy and campaigns team back in London. "We need to be on top of what is happening in Darfur. Are there genocidal aspects to this conflict? It already seems we are very late. How urgent is it? What should Aegis as an organization do? What should we as individuals do?"

The International Crisis Group had published a report a few months earlier, describing the conflict in Darfur that had come to a head one year earlier. It was complex, but the existence of a ruling elite that held a racist ideology towards the vulnerable, marginalized groups of black Africans suggested this might be more than just another conflict about power, resources, or land. Many aspects of the crisis pointed towards this being genocide, or very near to it: the deliberate destruction of a group because of their race, ethnicity, or religion.

The Darfur crisis has been emerging for years – long before the oppressed African tribes rose up in a rebellion in 2003 against the Arab government. It was one more crisis that followed a similar pattern in Sudan, of marginalized groups rebelling and the government of Sudan responding with crimes against humanity to subdue them. But in 2003–4, it grew significantly worse in the west, in Darfur.

~~Never Again!~~ Yet Again!

What later became a familiar story was then truly shocking. The government in Sudan mobilized militia, drawn from the Arab tribes. They armed and paid them to drive the African tribes off the land. They rode on horseback and in jeeps, burning villages, poisoning wells, killing men, and raping women. The government supported them with the Sudanese air force. Darfur saw indiscriminate aerial bombardment, scorched earth tactics which deliberately targeted civilians.

By 2005, around 300,000 people had perished and 3,000 villages had been destroyed – particularly those of the Fur, Masalit, and Zaghawa tribes. It also resulted in more than 2.5 million people being displaced into camps, mostly in Darfur, but also over the border in Chad and the Central African Republic.

There were well-documented fears of attacks, especially rape, for people leaving the refugee camps, to collect firewood for example. On the one hand, the displaced could not get out of the camps to find their own food; and on the other, humanitarian assistance was deliberately obstructed by the Khartoum regime, placing millions at risk of starvation.

On May 18, 2004, the *Times* of London ran an article by Aegis, authored by James – the first such article in the British press to describe what was happening in Darfur and state that it amounted to ethnic cleansing. "If they continue to obstruct the aid agencies and deliberately starve people," he wrote, "they will be guilty of committing genocide under the UN Convention." He also stated for the first time, in that and subsequent articles, the need to bring the perpetrators to account in the International Criminal Court (ICC). In mid-2004, this was a laughable prospect.

Because Sudan had not signed up to the court, it would require the United Nations Security Council to refer the situation in Darfur to the prosecutor of the ICC. This became a campaign that Aegis continued with a growing number of prominent organizations. The United States and China, opponents of the court, abstained instead of using their veto at the Security Council, allowing Resolution 1593 to pass in March 2005. Three years later, senior perpetrators of the Darfur crisis, including the

~~Never Again!~~ Yet Again!

president of Sudan, had been indicted. It won't happen quickly, but the cases of Slobodan Milosevic and Charles Taylor show that it is a matter of time before justice catches up and they stand in the dock.

As the crisis in Darfur continued from 2004 onwards, Aegis produced reports and briefings for the British Parliament and international diplomats, including a dossier in July 2005 about the kind of international operation that would be required to protect civilians in Darfur.

In 2005, Aegis brought together a group of Parliamentarians who became a permanent All-Party Parliamentary Group on Genocide Prevention. It was initially chaired by former Cabinet Minister Clare Short, and then by John Bercow, who was to become the Speaker of the British Parliament in 2009. At this point, Stephen Crabb took over as chairman. The group proved an effective tool to impact on policy. General Romeo Dallaire, the former head of the UN's peacekeeping mission in Rwanda in 1994, addressed the UK's Parliamentary Group on Genocide Prevention early in 2006 and, impressed, went on to found a similar group in Canada, where by then he was serving in the Senate.

Stephen Twigg, a minister in Tony Blair's government, lost his seat at the 2005 general election. He was a rising star, having unseated and brought an end to the political career of Michael Portillo, whom many had regarded as a future Conservative prime minister. Stephen's period out of politics was our gain. He joined the Aegis team as director of campaigns and policy, and would later chair the boards of both Aegis and the Holocaust Centre. He and James became frequent commentators on the Darfur crisis in the UK and international media.

The British and other governments emphasized that Darfur was a "humanitarian crisis," and they hid behind their generosity in sending aid. The Aegis Campaigns team worked successfully with the MPs on the Parliamentary Group to shift the discussion on Darfur from solely the need for aid to the need for security. Protecting civilians in times of crisis is politically much more

~~Never Again!~~ Yet Again!

difficult than sending food and setting up refugee camps, but the issue had to be firmly on the policy agenda of governments around the world.

While MPs and peers were raising Darfur in Parliament and organizing ministerial meetings, it became clear once again that to turn the political heat on the government, both the public and the media were needed. Aegis became a membership organization. Aside from contributing to projects supporting survivors in Rwanda and Darfur, Aegis members are encouraged to write to their MPs on specific issues. We witnessed how this grassroots campaign encouraged MPs to engage more with Darfur issues on the Parliamentary side of the campaign.

With encouragement from the Pears Foundation in the UK, Aegis started the "Protect Darfur" campaign, which organized the first public rallies outside Downing Street. We timed them to coincide with the US rallies of the Save Darfur Coalition, with whom Aegis worked closely. Later, as we focused more on the policy and media work, coordination of the street events shifted to the Globe for Darfur, which was a loose coalition of organizations funded by the US Save Darfur Coalition, and based in the Aegis office for a year before other coalition members took responsibility. We worked with colleagues in other non-governmental organizations in the USA, Europe, and Asia to secure the best strategic partnerships for levering political awareness. Aegis members remained active in the campaigns, especially the regular Globe for Darfur rallies outside Downing Street, held at the same time as events in up to forty countries around the world.

The most active campaigners were students. The Aegis Students movement was born in 2005 with the first Society at Oxford University. Three years later, there were twelve Aegis Student Societies. Their mission is to educate informally and engage young people with genocide issues through the screening of films, and holding debates and talks in universities. They also fund-raise for vulnerable survivors in Rwanda and Darfur and take part in the campaigns when needed. The Aegis Students'

~~Never Again!~~ Yet Again!

greatest success was advocating on behalf of Darfuris who had reached the shores of the UK, believing they had reached a place of safety.

The British government's current guidance on Darfuri asylum cases makes it extremely difficult to secure asylum simply on the basis of persecution in Sudan as a non-Arab. The country guidance for Sudan advised that as the Darfur crisis is in the west of the country, it is safe to deport Darfuris back to other parts of Sudan. This means that people who have survived the burning of their villages and the murder of their families in the western province of Darfur will be returned to the capital, Khartoum, from where the violence is orchestrated and the brutal security apparatus is based. After the Evian Conference in 1938, when free countries turned their backs on fleeing Jews, seventy years later, we still have policies that close the doors to the victims of racist ideologies, for fear that the victims may overrun us, or because we are afraid of the political fallout if we confront genocidal regimes. It's not just the asylum seekers that suffer. It gives a dangerous signal to the perpetrating government that we turn a blind eye, or do not care about their victims.

While the students campaigned for individuals, there were some 500 Darfuris at risk of deportation and we set out to challenge UK government policy – first in the media, with films and stories. It became a national story on Channel 4, BBC's *Newsnight*, and a number of national newspapers.

At the same time, we knew this battle had to be won in the courts, so we sent investigators to Sudan to gather evidence of torture of those Darfuris who had been forcibly returned. The campaign to overturn this policy has been taken all the way to the House of Lords on appeal. The Darfuris lost on a point of law, so a fresh case had been brought. By 2009, the Home Office continued to delay the tribunal hearings – we hope because they know there is a body of evidence against their inhuman policy. As long as there is a delay, it keeps the Darfuris safe, so the tactic is working to a degree; but without a decision from the tribunal, they also hover in an uncertain future.

~~Never Again!~~ Yet Again!

Genocidaires are so convinced by their ideologies that they are prepared to kill innocent people for them. Such is their conviction that they will fly in the face of all human morals, common sense, and international law. Trying to reason with them is really not an option. Nor should it be an option to allow them to operate with total impunity on the basis that the bigger the crime, the more likely they are to get away with it. Aegis takes the view that it is in the interest of the victims to pursue the issue of justice vigorously, while the crimes are ongoing. The International Criminal Court has been established to do just that, but it also needs the support of organizations that act on behalf of the victims at grassroots level. Victims know more about their victimization than anyone else and can help their own cause, given the right support.

Out of our work to document and collect evidence emerged our program on international justice, headed by Nick Donovan, who used to work in the prime minister's strategy unit. The Aegis team scored a major victory in its campaign to strengthen British law on genocide, war crimes, and crimes against humanity. Aegis has carefully documented two major loopholes in British law on international crimes, and has drafted a new bill to close this gap. One of these loopholes was that people can only be prosecuted for genocide, war crimes, and crimes against humanity if they committed those crimes *after 2001*. This does not cover those suspected of involvement, for instance, in the Rwandan genocide, or in the atrocities committed in Bosnia. This means that the UK has become a safe haven for perpetrators of genocide from Rwanda and other situations. On July 7, 2009, the UK government announced that it was going to backdate jurisdiction to *January 1991*. This announcement was a direct result of Aegis' media and parliamentary campaign to strengthen the law in this area.

Nick brought top-flight lawyers into the Wanted for War Crimes project, initiated by Aegis in 2009. In some respects, it is a continuation of the work of the Simon Wiesenthal Center, targeting perpetrators of more contemporary crimes against humanity. The primary objective is to create a network of NGOs,

~~Never Again!~~ Yet Again!

investigators, lawyers, and other groups willing to share information and evidence about people suspected of war crimes, torture, crimes against humanity, or genocide; and to help build prima facie cases against suspects, so that national police and investigators can quickly obtain an arrest warrant or make an extradition request. A secondary objective is to work with a wide coalition of groups and actors willing to pressure UN member states, the Security Council, the European Union, and, through these institutions, other governments, to arrest suspects for whom the International Criminal Court and tribunals have issued arrest warrants.

This is happening as I write. It is not fifteen years ago, twenty-five years ago, or half a century ago. As I put the coffee on, the people who are the perpetrators of the atrocities in Darfur are maintaining the cordon of their successful ethnic cleansing. The recent victims of bombings, widowhood, or gang rape are suffering unnecessary pain at this very moment. The lawyers and politicians may argue about definitions and international law – whether to label the crime genocide or crimes against humanity – but we all know that a government is targeting innocent civilians because of who they are. What is important, on the one hand, is that there is resolve to bring them to account, to stop the impunity that allows them to commit the same crimes again and again. But on the other, we also need to learn how to act earlier to stop the violence in the first place, and when it does happen, to foster the political will to protect those at risk.

For genocide prevention to be effective, we have to deploy a whole range of strategies that no single organization, agency, or government can achieve alone. It has to be deep collaboration, with compassion and tactical strength playing equal roles, and with political will driving the deployment of strategies that actually have effect. If there is one thing we know about prevention ten years into our work in that field, it is that it is really easy to talk the talk, because nothing is easier to condemn. It is also extremely difficult to walk the walk, because almost certainly you will have to make political decisions that will not be popular, either with

~~Never Again!~~ YET AGAIN!

the electorate or with other strategic partners – and you will have to take action in territory that is of absolutely no strategic or economic interest whatsoever. It really is a humanitarian role, but not one that readily pulls the heartstrings of the electorate or media. So resolve is required. And resolve is in short supply. Or so we have discovered.

Chapter Twenty
The Future of Memory

The trajectory of memory is changing rapidly. The generation that experienced the Holocaust is still with us, but it is fading fast. Memory is rapidly turning to history. With the passing of the baton, a significant change is taking place. Whatever we have heard, whatever evidence we have collected, whatever we have been told, the way in which we discuss this history in years to come, the way in which we discuss the Holocaust, will be very different without the survivor generation who have spoken to us firsthand. We all know that. But the question is, "What will the memory be fifty years from now?"

Fifty years from now, the facts will not have changed. The Holocaust will still be what it is today. We may in fact know more, because by then we will have been able to make more use of the archives that we have available to us to write the history more fully, more accurately. This history is very unusual in that it was supposed to be secret, but the perpetrators left a smoking gun, with millions of pieces of evidence that they had inadvertently produced in their meticulous pursuit of perfection, or had just omitted to destroy.

Ironically, the Nazis intended to wipe out the Jews without exception, but with a slip of inefficiency, they created several hundred thousand Jewish survivors who could stand as eyewitnesses to their audacious plan. Their biggest mistake of all was Auschwitz. They created the largest killing facility in the Third

~~Never Again!~~ Yet Again!

Reich, then for some reason selected around ten percent of Jews who arrived there to work in the camp or in other work camps. These Jews arrived at the camp and either had long enough to see the gas chambers, or were even taken to the camp and set to work. It gave them just long enough to see everything, before being deported to a sub-camp or work camp in an altogether different part of the Third Reich. It did not happen in Belzec, Treblinka, Chelmno, or Sobibor, where inmates were either gassed or were among a very few selected for the *Sonderkommando*. And so Auschwitz-Birkenau produced the very thing it was there to eliminate – eyewitnesses.

Of course, those eyewitnesses were only a fraction of those who encountered National Socialism and its persecution in some way. But they were significant in one particular way. They were witnesses to genocide, and the whole intent of genocide is to murder without exception and to remove the threat of witnesses to the crime. We have many such witnesses.

One of the ways in which we have constructed a totally unique record of the Holocaust is because eyewitnesses have contributed to our knowledge. The Nazis left behind a significant amount of documentation; the Soviets collected documents; the courts also amassed an important amount of documentary evidence; and the international tracing service has millions of documents. So the written record of the crimes is immense. But in this case, the crimes were committed against individuals based on their ethnicity. This means that some nine million Jews were targeted individually because of their group membership. Many fled to safer zones and avoided the worst excesses. Around six million did not make it through the genocidal onslaught. A small number made it through some, or all, of the occupation of the Nazis and survived to tell the story. But that small number was enough to provide a significant body of evidence about what it meant to be a Jew living and surviving in Nazi territory. Not all by any means made it through Auschwitz or one of the other death camps. Many were in concentration camps, or labor camps, or work factories. Some were in hiding, on the run, or assumed

The Future of Memory

false identities. Some lived in areas that were occupied for a relatively short period of time. Whatever the experience of those who survived, they had a unique insight, because without exception they were targeted for murder and the full force of the Nazi regime was out to eliminate them. They were the exception rather than rule, but so huge was the plan to eliminate the Jews that the small remnant of survivors is a group drawn from over twenty countries, speaking more than twenty languages.

The genius of Steven Spielberg was not in recognizing that the Holocaust survivors were a significant group of people with a huge story to tell the world; nor in recognizing that they were elderly and would not be around forever to tell their story. His genius actually lay in knowing that taking their video-testimonies wherever they were around the world was possible, that it would make an indelible contribution to knowledge and understanding, and that it absolutely needed to be done for posterity.

When the Survivors of the Shoah Visual History Foundation was created in 1994, it soon received the working name The Spielberg Archive. Survivors called it that; scholars called it that; students called it that. Spielberg never called it that. He was too interested in its real global significance to call it that. He only wanted to know how the survivors' voices would be heard in the long term through the archive. Over several years, starting in 1994, it collected 51,682 Holocaust survivor testimonies from 56 countries around the world, and in 32 languages. Today, the testimonies are a part of the University of Southern California in Los Angeles, a respected research and teaching university, where they are kept in perpetuity. The testimonies are catalogued and indexed, and used by researchers to explore the detail of the Holocaust experience through the words of those who were really there. This may not seem like such a big task, but the preservation of the testimonies has been a multimillion-dollar project. It is now a state-of-the-art collection, with the benefit of sophisticated search facilities to assist with research and education.

Personal testimony has its limitations. As Primo Levi stated, memory is a "fallacious instrument." We can only remember what

~~Never Again!~~ YET AGAIN!

we can remember – which means that at times we do not remember everything. The Shoah Foundation Institute archive is, therefore, remarkable for its accuracy, not because everything has been remembered accurately, but for just how much has been remembered at all, and for the levels of accuracy achieved, considering the passage of time. What the Shoah Foundation Institute has achieved is documenting a huge and indisputable repository of testimony, running to 105,000 hours of recorded interviews. This in itself is a significant contribution to knowledge and makes clear that testimony is a documentary source in its own right.

The biggest decision I have made in my career is to leave the Holocaust Centre, Aegis, and the Holocaust Memorial Day Trust – all organizations I helped to found – to move to Los Angeles and take up the position of Executive Director at USC Shoah Foundation Institute. It is not the distance that makes the move a big one. We live in a world small enough for relocation to Los Angeles to be relatively local. The real question is, why would you leave organizations that are vibrant, fresh, and highly driven to go to a large university with an archive? The answer is very simple. The Shoah Foundation Institute's collection is the single largest body of visual history on any subject in the world. It creates an indisputable case for studying the Holocaust. It also makes a case for documenting histories of a similar nature, such as those experienced in Rwanda, Bosnia, and other genocidal situations. If we want to make a powerful case for the need to learn respect, to overcome racism, to work on the prevention of genocide, how better to do that than to collect the testimony of survivors of the Holocaust and genocide, and to make those voices heard the world over? They are the compelling voice of conscience that tells us clearly what the consequences are if we ignore the warnings from history.

The USC Shoah Foundation Institute has a vital role in giving voice to the future. To be custodian of that collection for just a short time in its long, long history to come, and to have the opportunity to illuminate what USC Provost Max Nikias calls "timeless truths" – before we even know just how timeless they

The Future of Memory

are – is an immense honor. In that archive, there are the memories not only of 51,682 survivors, but also of all the families they represent, and all the generations that follow.

Just imagine if someone had tape-recorded the Jews after the Nuremberg Laws in 1935, or after *Kristallnacht* in 1938, or maybe in the Warsaw ghetto in 1941, or in Plaszow in 1943, or in Bergen-Belsen in 1944. What kind of impact might those recordings have had? What kind of memory would we have now? Moreover, if that testimony, collected in real time, had been made available, how compelling might it have been? Do you see where I am heading? If the testimony was collected in real time and made available to the leaders of the world as a compelling voice, could the victims themselves have been the voice that changed history? Of course, it is totally naive to think that would have been the case, but we know for sure that victims understand their victimization better than anyone else. It does not need fifty years of silence to articulate what the victims felt at the time. The facts are the same; the human experience is arguably stronger at the time.

Now take the world in which we live. Imagine that you could hear the voices of the current victims of genocide unfolding in real time. Could we make a compelling statement to help turn the tide of aggression against them? At the very least, could we not make those voices heard, to those who want to hear?

The real words of real people who have encountered – or are encountering – the effects of hatred and genocide have a powerful and penetrating message. The real question is how to channel their silent voices into voices with the power to change the outcome of their own situation.

Chapter Twenty-One
Inconclusive

We still live in a world in which we might despair, a world in which the fragile beauty of living is senselessly shattered over and over again. A world in which terms like freedom, innocence, love, care, hope, peace, and goodness are in the vocabulary of all, but not in the experience of enough. A world driven by material greed, political power, and disregard for all but those inside the immediate circle in which we live. As we protect ourselves in our safe environments, even now somebody nearby is hurting from the effects of prejudice, abuse, or blatant victimization. And somehow we have to live in this world. Somehow we must make it work.

When we dare to look back, we see a past littered with massacres, with crying children and ruined civilizations. When we reflect upon our present, we see how quickly, indeed how easily, we identify enemies, real or imagined. Time and again, we create the conditions in which we justify driving our neighbors from their homes, raping their women, and killing their sons. Sometimes, depending on the circumstances, we call it war; at other times, genocide or ethnic cleansing. You may call it what you like, but when people are killed in the name of ideology, territory, power, race, or religion, we have wasted lives. We have murdered someone who was meant to live, to enjoy everything that is beautiful about human existence and to die in peace. But then, within our troubled imaginations and paranoid temperaments, we justify, excuse, and cover the cracks of the past. And then when we look

~~Never Again!~~ Yet Again!

to the future, just over the horizon we know that sooner or later, someone else will become the victim of another's deluded fantasies. Somewhere, right now, there are ordinary people with ordinary lives, who, unbeknown to them, will soon become the victims of the next round of racial hate and persecution.

It is a deeply disturbing reality. This failure to arrest our impulse to inhumanity over and over again leads me toward a troubling cynicism. It taunts me to believe that the human condition cannot change. The senseless repetition of degrading and murderous injustices leads me to believe that pain and suffering and hurting hearts are an almost inevitable and integral part of human existence. And sadly, perhaps it's true.

But then, once in a while, in the midst of this debacle that we call civilization, there is something that can give us hope and a means to move forward. Something that enables us to see our way more clearly. In that moment, part of our past is made clear and the way to the future made more plausible. Perhaps we are afforded a glimpse into the dark soul of humanity, but given in some form the means to confront it. Such moments should bring us together, bridge our divided past, and create the means to a shared and meaningful future for people of all backgrounds, faiths, and convictions. In establishing the Holocaust Centre, Beth Shalom, we wanted to provide a place where a moment of such hope might be created for those who come. Not to gloss the past, but to confront it, and find our way through the confusion of despair.

It would be good to say that we speak on behalf of the victims, "so that their lives were not in vain." But of course, it was all in vain because nothing can be gained from a tragedy so absolute, so soul-destroying and so final. The lives of the Jews of Europe were wasted; so too were those slain in Bosnia and Rwanda and East Timor, and in Guatemala and Cambodia. They were people and they were destroyed, and there is nothing more wasteful than wasting human life. Imagine it was you. Not some other person, but you. Just imagine that it was your life that was about to be extinguished for some ideological end. Would it matter then? That's the point. Every life is worth living. Certainly no one has

Inconclusive

the right to destroy in wanton, cold blood. In honor of the wasted lives strewn around us, we strive to learn about what they went through; and through their voices we do what we can to learn from it, too. Learning from it means taking whatever the "lessons" are and ensuring that we put them into practice, without prejudice and every time. We talk of the "lessons" of the Holocaust as if it were self-evident that "it" should not occur again. But that is not a lesson. That is our hope. The lessons lie in what we are prepared to do. And so the question is, what are we actually prepared to do?

We are involved in a search to salvage something. It does not mean that the lives lost will be found again, or that those who weep will find the solace they desire, and surely deserve. It does not mean that anything that is past can be relived for a better outcome. Clearly, it cannot be. It means that in spite of the despair, in spite of the broken hearts, in spite of the destruction and devastation, in spite of it all, the will to create a meaningful – if not hopeful – future can be found. It should be a future in which common understanding, compassion, and care are shared across the boundaries of culture, religion, and ethnicity.

We must be realistic. No single person, place, or group of people is enough to effect the change that we need. In our varied organizations, in our religious institutions, in our homes and hearts, we often repeat the words "Never Again!" The sincerity of this should never be called into question. But what we mean by these words, and what we are prepared to do to ensure that they become more than a cliché, is something we must continue to ask ourselves. In creating the Holocaust Centre, one of our goals was to contribute to ensuring that such things are not repeated. But the means to do so lies not in the cliché itself, but in talking, discussing, and learning; in the choices we make, and in changing the way we behave toward one another.

And so the journey we began in Jerusalem continues. It is a journey that has confronted us with many challenging and troubling facts about human existence. It has tested our human endurance, our Christian identity, our sense of past, present, and future; but most of all, it has made us think about who we are,

~~Never Again!~~ Yet Again!

what we want to be, and what kind of world we want to pass on to our children.

I described much earlier my sense of utter devastation on visiting the mass grave at Zbylitowska Gora, and the feeling that we inhabit a broken world. The despair will never leave us; it is the despair of those who can never be consoled. I have come to recognize, however, that there is an opportunity to think about the Jewish concept of *tikkun olam* – to mend the world. During the Middle Ages, it was thought that the intercession of the sages could bring about the reinstitution of the Temple in Jerusalem. Alas! That did not happen. Today, *tikkun olam* requires people of all walks of life to face the destruction that has happened in our time, and to go on to create a world of peace; to listen to pain and anguish, and to find someone to console. It is to see the abandonment of the Jews as the abandonment of humanity, and then always to remain vigilant. It is to see the hatred, and to create understanding. It is to see the loss, and to create a world in which everyone is valued for who they are.

In the memorial hall at the Holocaust Centre, we chose to put the words "He who saves a single life, saves the world entire," from Pirkei Avot in the Talmud. These words were chosen for several reasons. Firstly, so that when we are working with people from across the spectrum of British life, of all ages and backgrounds, as we study the history of the Holocaust, we can further ask, "What difference might it have made if more people had been prepared to speak out and to save even a single neighbor or friend?" By extension, we could also ask, "What difference might the avoidance of indifference make in our world today?"

The other reason we chose to put that all-important text around our hall was more personal. It was so that every time I went into that hall – which for fifteen years was virtually every day of my life – I also asked myself the question, "Would you have been courageous enough to do that…and, more importantly, are you?"

The struggle is not about how not to forget, but about how to remember and to make it count. "Never again!" is already "Yet again!" That would be fine if it did not represent the real loss of

INCONCLUSIVE

real lives, and the real pain and trauma suffered by so many. It is not fine; it is not good; it is not acceptable. Because there is something that we can do. There are many things we can do, which generally we do not do.

There is nothing I would like to do more than leave you with a sense of empowerment and the feeling that you really can do something.

Yesterday I had lunch with Ilee Rhimes, the vice-provost at USC for information technology. He is a brilliant man who is able to use his technical skills to run a powerful computer center, where the Shoah Foundation Institute's testimonies are housed. He said to me, "Much of my computing work is rather mundane. But when I work with the Shoah Foundation testimonies, I have the feeling that my everyday computing skills could be making a real difference." Rhimes struck a very real chord with me. He would be running the Information Technology Services Department at USC anyway, but he was prepared to use his position and his skills to make a real difference. Herein lies the secret. None of us can make a significant enough difference to change the world on our own. But having the commitment to recognize where and how our skills *can* make a real difference is what ultimately will make the step change that we all want.

It is not over. Men, women, and children will die in callous acts of violence before our eyes for generations to come. We will struggle with the reality of that; we will wish for better things. Unfortunately, we do not have the apparatus, the capacity, or the will to resolve every conflict and every act of genocide that is occurring on our planet. And so it will not end now – which means there are mothers, fathers, sisters, and brothers who are about to become the victims of the next round of madness, who are not yet victims, and whose lives could be lived. We need to prevent their lives from being wasted. I often think, what if the next life was yours, what lengths would you be prepared to go to? Do we make the same effort, or anything like it, for others?

It's inconclusive. "Never again!" has resulted in initiatives, research, and attempts to intervene. There is a body of text which

~~Never Again!~~ Yet Again!

criticizes foreign policy and intervention strategies. We know our shortcomings and our failures. But what we are really prepared to do is inconclusive.

That leaves this book inconclusive, too. Was it worthwhile attempting to remember in a meaningful way, if there was no real commitment to change? Was it worth rallying thousands of people to use their voice if they were unlikely to be heard? Was it really worth the hope that something would change, when nothing appears to have changed?

The answer has to be that it *was* worth it, though little has changed and nothing is certain. If we do not struggle with the causes and consequences of genocide, and if we are not prepared to fail, then there will never be any change. There really is no reason why genocide and government-sponsored mass killing need to continue. In the meantime, we keep telling the story and remembering, not for memory's sake alone, but as a reminder.

Because we do not need to remember.

We need to be reminded.